UNLEASHED!

How a Lost Dog Rescued a Lost Love

MICHAEL GUERIN

Diartspora Press

Wynnewood, PA

Disclaimer: Although all of the events in this book are true, some names have been changed.

Cover photos: Katie Pfeiffer

ISBN: 978-0-578-31990-2 (paperback)
ISBN: 978-0-578-32744-0 (eBook)

Library of Congress Control Number: 2021922506

Diartspora Press LLC
P.O. Box 117
Wynnewood, PA 19096

DEDICATION

This book is dedicated to the amazing men and women who give so freely of their time and energy to care for and rescue creatures of all kinds. Their tireless efforts serve to heal not just the animals in need, but, often, their owners as well.

ACKNOWLEDGEMENTS

It takes a village to not only find a missing pet, but to write a book about it as well. Katie and I owe a huge debt of gratitude to Tammy Feby, who made our desperate cause to find ZeeZee her own, mobilizing an incredible team who joined in our search. Kevin, Michelle, Sharon, Randy, Eric, Dann—we are in your debt.

A special thank-you goes out to Dann Furia. He refused to let physical limitations stop him from using his indispensable knowledge of the terrain to continually search for and eventually find ZeeZee. Without him, this story would have a much sadder ending indeed.

I got a lot of help getting this story into print. Another big thank-you goes to Bruce Hulse—model, photographer, fellow scribe and sought-after sensei. His constant support and encouragement kept me motivated throughout the writing process. The final outcome was immeasurably aided by the adept editing and informed feedback of Alan Nevins and Jacklyn Saferstein. Their contributions through six re-writes were enormous.

I also owe a debt of gratitude to my sister, Marisa Guerin, who can add "skilled copy editor" to her illustrious resume. Thank you, Seesa. And many thanks to Liz Loverro, who did everything necessary to design, format, and basically birth the manuscript into the world of print. Love you, Liz.

Lastly, and most importantly, I want to express my deep gratitude to Katie Pfeiffer. From start to finish, pushing past fatigue and fear, it was her unceasing drive and focus that ultimately resulted in ZeeZee's successful rescue. It was due to her social media efforts that we found Tammy and her team. Katie's actions and instincts throughout our ordeal were always right on target.

Katie saved ZeeZee's life. Twice. And mine once.

What can I say? Thank you. For everything.

UNLEASHED!

How a Lost Dog Rescued a Lost Love

CHAPTER ONE

I never wanted a dog.

When I got the dog I never wanted, I fell in love with her.

That's what got me into trouble. If she hadn't wormed and squirmed her way into my heart, I might have endured the tragedy that befell me and my partner Katie much better. The tragedy was that our beloved Chihuahua ZeeZee was lost by our pet sitter. On the first day of what was to be a rare vacation. In an area far from home and rife with predators. For twelve long, hot, trying days. Oh, and without wearing her tags. This is the story of how ZeeZee came to us, how she left us, and how we got her back. And how the paranormal and the generosity of animal lovers played a part in her recovery.

It is also the story of something else that was lost and then found. Love. How Katie and I frittered it away, and how we found it during our search for Zees. As a wise man said, it's easy to get lost; all you have to do is lose your perspective. We were guilty as charged. But in coming together to rescue another—even one with four legs instead of two—we not only found our precious canine daughter, but re-discovered our own deep connection as well. All thanks to the dog I never wanted.

There might have been one more thing that I found. Me. Yes, me. Granted, I depart from being my genuine self perhaps dozens…make that hundreds…of times daily. That's life in the big world for you. But what I went through in those twelve body, mind, and soul-scorching days devoted to finding a needle in a haystack, a sick and scared animal on the run in strange surroundings, had the side effect of placing me face to face with my self. My capital S Self. That one I seem to always ignore, but can never ultimately evade.

But let's begin at the beginning.

Yes, it's true; I never wanted a dog. I never wanted cats, either, but you wouldn't have guessed that from the four felines that prowled the tiny apartment shared by Katie and me several years ago. Boofy was the first; a diffident and difficult orange tabby who was loved by the other cats almost as much as he disliked humans. Boofy was followed by Dali, Blackie, and the beloved Hugo. These wonderful and unexpected creatures each somehow found a way into our home, and, inevitably, into our hearts. Their loving companionship and just plain adorableness melted my resistance to owning major arcana mammals, and paved the way for ZeeZee's eventual arrival.

How we managed to share our cramped quarters with even one cat, let alone four, defies credulity. Then again, defying credulity is something at which Katie and I were experts, from the very start. After all, we owed our first, fateful meeting not to chance or a plan of any kind, but to a prompt from the beyond.

We met one night at a popular bistro on the outskirts of Oakland. I was with a friend, as was she. Katie and I sometimes joke that if the seating arrangements had been different that evening, we both might have been in different relationships all these years. But the odds that we met at all were highly improbable. That's because Katie and her friend had been to that same bistro just the week before and decided they didn't like it much. Thought it was too snooty. Too full of posers. Posers like me and my friend, I guess.

And yet, on that particular July night, Katie was possessed with an overwhelming sense that she had to go there again. She didn't really know why. Her friend was mystified. She knew Katie wasn't prone to giving places or people a second chance. All that Katie knew was that when she thought of the place, it "lit up." That is the way she describes the flashes of intuition which burst upon her consciousness with amazing regularity; things "light up" for her. Often, they may not make sense. Sense comes from somewhere else. But Katie learned from long experience that ignoring such illuminations was always a mistake.

She had been having these mysterious moments of precognition ever since attending a weekend retreat focusing on creativity while in art school. Her group was lying in a circle on the floor with eyes closed, listening to self-hypnosis tapes by the pioneering out-of-body researcher Robert Monroe. On the second day, on tape thirteen, Katie had a vision. She saw another member of the group, a young woman she didn't know, in a room. When the exercise was over, Katie went over to her and relayed everything she had perceived: how both the room and the woman's roommate looked, what was transpiring, and how the issue was resolved. The more she talked, the wider the woman's eyes grew. This was getting a little too eerie.

"How could you know that? Have you been to my place? Are you spying on me? Do we know each other from somewhere?"

The answer to all of the above was no. It was just information that came to Katie; she didn't know how or why. For the rest of the weekend, she continued to see images explode around people's faces, and when she shared what she was picking up, each person had the same, dumbfounded reaction. It was uncanny. Somehow, the tapes had caused a sort of psychic awakening in Katie; a gift which has persisted to this day. And it was in response to that inner guidance that she insisted to her friend that they needed to return to that same, pretentious cafe that fateful evening; who knew why? Time to meet more posers!

I remember the place being crowded that night. There were no empty tables, but there were some tables with empty seats. Perfect conditions for meeting new people. If one had a little gumption, that is. Which is why I came with Serge. Left to my own devices, I probably would have stood in a corner, nursing a series of drinks and perfecting an air of benign savoir faire, while silently praying that someone, anyone, would offer me a seat.

Serge was an old—and I do mean old—pro at the chatting-females-up game. I had to hand it to him. He wasn't about to let his missing follicles, sallow skin and stubborn halitosis deprive women the opportunity to get to know him. He made a beeline for Katie's table and asked if we could join them. She and her friend were gracious and said yes.

I sat next to Katie. This was a major stroke of luck. Her friend was attractive, but no match for Katie's striking features and luminous personality. I found myself staring at a beaming young woman with cropped hair the color of roasted coffee beans and the most beautiful, almond-shaped, hazel eyes I had ever seen. If eyes are indeed the window of the soul, hers were bay windows; her inner essence with all its passion on full display. I was mesmerized.

There is a scripture from the East which consists of a series of questions from a student to the Master. One of them suddenly came to mind. "Who is a hero?" The answer? "A hero is he who flinches not when faced with the arrows which fly from the eyes of a beautiful woman."

Now that's an answer. And I know exactly what the Master was intimating. I got it. But apparently, my hero days still lay ahead of me. I flinched.

We started to chat. And then to talk. And then to discuss. And then on and on to deeper and deeper levels of sharing and communication. The conversation flowed effortlessly. We discovered we liked some of the same books, films, and art. I learned that she was a graduate of the prestigious San Francisco Institute of Art. And, that she was psychic! She shared how things "lit up" for her, and how that gift came about. She learned that I had my own business. And one more thing about me that took her by surprise, and has been key to our connection ever since.

Katie was amazed to discover that this older, worldly-seeming guy sipping a chardonnay actually shared her awareness of and interest in all things spiritual. She seemed taken aback by the ease with which I could speak knowledgeably about the concepts of chi and chakras, karma and Kundalini. She was even more intrigued to find out that my acquaintanceship with them was not limited to the theoretical.

As it happened, I spent the decade of my twenties living a monkish existence in an ashram. The word means "shelter" in Hindi, and, indeed, it was that. Observing poverty, chastity, and obedience is one way not to fall victim to the maya (illusion) occasioned by greed, lust, and power. But the real focus was the daily practice of techniques for going within. I had many profound and beautiful experiences during those years that I never would have encountered any other way. I had also read more than my share of spiritual books, which, let the record state, were usually more prone to confuse than enlighten. Concepts are no substitute for direct experience. Still, they granted me familiarity with the great variety of belief systems which all tried to "eff the Ineffable."

Maybe that's what made it easy talking to Katie. Maybe we were just two old souls catching up with each other; picking up from whenever it was we left off. It wasn't always easy for me to play the dating game. Let me correct that…it was never easy. I was always shy. The Catholic high school I attended was separated into a boy's side and a girl's side. I only had one co-ed class in four years, and I didn't have the moxie that some guys had to go over and talk to girls during our mutual recess time. I had plenty of crushes, but no dates and no girl friends. My presence at school dances had only one apparent purpose: to lean firmly up against the cinderblock walls so as to save folks in the event of an earthquake. I left the dancing, co-mingling, and, well, fun, to others.

A while after my ashram years ended, I was fortunate to meet a lovely woman who came into my life at just the right time and who made it easy for me to enter that most mysterious of realms—a relationship! We were together for a few years before splitting up, but remained friends. My dating skills remained rusty, hence Serge. But now conversing and connecting with

Katie was easy. Hours passed like minutes. There were no nerves. And that was a good sign.

We shared telephone numbers. Serge had to go somewhere and he was my ride, so we said our good-byes and headed out the door.

It was when I turned around outside on the sidewalk to look back at the cafe that it was my turn to be surprised. And to learn something about myself which was difficult to accept.

I saw Katie and her friend exiting the bistro and walking under the street lamps in the other direction, away from us. It was then I saw that she was wearing a pair of multi-colored and striped leggings which would not have looked out of place in the wardrobe department of Ringling Brothers. They were positively luminescent. I hadn't noticed them previously because she had been sitting the whole time; her legs were hidden beneath the table. From a fashion standpoint, I thought they were pretty shocking stockings. My own sartorial palette is much more restrained. Practically everything I own would be perfect camouflage if I had to blend in with a mud wall.

But it wasn't Katie's leggings which gave me pause.

I watched and saw for the first time the somewhat ungainly, slightly swaying gait I would later become so familiar with; an arrhythmic stride caused by her shortened and weakened left leg. Katie suffered significant nerve damage while she was being birthed, and it affected the entire left side of her body. It hadn't been noticeable to me at the table. It was now. And it affected me.

I couldn't help wondering: would I have been quite so eager to get to know this same wonderful woman had she lumberingly approached me on the street with her Crayola-colored ensemble on full display? Would I have fallen victim to an instant prejudice due to some unconscious, goofy societal programming and avoided her? Or would I have been centered enough to reserve judgement, to be open to her amazing presence, and to engage with her as zealously as I had in the cafe?

It's a hypothetical question with only hypothetical answers possible. But it is a question raised twenty-eight years ago. We have been together and I have been regularly flinching ever since. We never officially tied The Knot, but are inextricably linked by a million smaller ones. And we have yet to run out of things to say.

As we got to know each other, we discovered we had something else in common besides our mutual interest in exploring what lies within. It was something not quite as edifying. In fact, it was dismal. And it might have explained why neither of us had a cat or dog or any other kind animal when we met. It took a while to come out, because it wasn't something of which either of us was proud.

Turns out, we both had a history of lethal pet ownership. No other way to put it. To be sure, we were both children at the time, but that doesn't make it any more acceptable. And it was something that affected us both, even into adulthood.

Not every child is blessed to grow up with an animal as a friend. And among those that do, not every pet is of the warm-blooded variety. Or the kind with fur. Some kids have to content themselves with stroking something in a shell. Or with scales. Or feathers. Some pets you can't handle or play with; only watch from behind glass or in front of a wire cage. Some pets need to be fed creatures which other people might consider pets. Maybe sometimes, it's the child that makes these pet choices. But a lot of times, I suspect, it's the parents.

Case in point: me. I grew up in a family with five sisters, one brother. and, for much of the time, zero animals. Each of my siblings pleaded with my Dad to be allowed to get a puppy. I, for some reason, didn't. And now I think I know why...I didn't know what I was missing! That's because not a single household on either side of the street where I grew up owned a dog. There were lots and lots of kids, but no puppies. No cats either, for that matter. Squirrels were the only mammals around, and they weren't really pet material.

Subsequently, I never knew the joys of rough-housing with a furry, four-legged friend. Never played fetch, never clung to a canine for comfort while crying my eyes out, never got sprayed by a dog shaking its wet fur, never laughed when a cold wet snout mashed up against my own, and never felt the ticklish joys of getting a face-licking from the only creature in the universe likely to worship me. I just didn't know such heart-warming experiences existed.

Whenever one of my siblings brought up the puppy request, inspired by who knows what, my father would always have the same response. Normally the most reserved, calm, and taciturn of men, his eyes would widen, an excited smile would stretch across his face, and in the most enthusiastic tone of voice imaginable, he would exclaim "Let's not and say we did!"

This was to become his default response to any request he knew was doomed to failure. And he almost had us! We were always taken in by his instant exuberance. A moment later, however, we realized we weren't completely sold on the idea. Somehow, the notion of not getting what we wanted but saying we did never seemed as equally satisfying as actually getting what we wanted. But I guess it was his way of letting us down easy, and over the years it eventually became a family joke.

Of course, my father was himself privileged to own a dog when he was a kid growing up in South Philadelphia. All right, so he lived in a much smaller household. But to live in the urban environment down by Broad and Wolf streets was to live pretty far from any evidence of the natural world. All the nearby fields were made of concrete and asphalt.

And yet he and his two sisters had a dog! This fact belied the image of the strict, no-nonsense household run by my grandmother we were led to believe. But, to be fair, I think Dad viewed the prospect of adding a four-legged friend to our already crowded house in the suburbs to be so daunting that, in the end, he decreed that all pets must be kept to the cold-blooded variety.

Sure, he might have relented and allowed one of us to have a hamster or something, just to try and keep the peace, but then what? For all he knew, that hamster might be the gateway mammal, and, next thing you know, there would be a herd of ponies grazing in our backyard.

So, reptiles and fish it was. Dime store turtles placidly plodding to and fro in their tiny plastic tropical paradise; complete with palm tree and desert island. The place to go to back in the early sixties if you wanted to purchase some non-native, exotic, legally dubious species of animal was at your friendly neighborhood Woolworth's. The quintessential five and dime. You could go in there looking for fish liver oil, come across some fishing line, have a tuna fish sandwich at the lunch counter, and leave with a couple of angelfish swimming in a plastic bag. The entire breadth of evolution was for sale; from plants to snails, serpents and fish. From turtles and reptiles to birds, and on to mammals. The small, prey variety. The check-out girl at the register obviously represented the crown of creation. At least to my pubescent eyes.

That's where I got my turtles. These guys were so lacking in observable personality traits that I don't think we even bothered to give them individual names. They were beautiful, however, with intersecting red and yellow lines patterned throughout their swamp-green bulk. One of them seemed partial to rock music, solemnly swaying to and fro to the Stones "Satisfaction." I don't know if he ever got any, but I used to get a lot just looking into its eerie, enigmatic eyes. Warm blooded, they definitely weren't.

Then, for a while, I got into tropical fish. There's a reason they can be found in a lot of dentist's waiting rooms. You can't help but become tranquilized, watching these brilliantly colored creatures drifting and darting in and out of the gently waving fronds and sea grasses. A salt water tank was beyond my reach then, but I did my best with my meager resources to stock a vibrant, fresh-water tank. I paid visits to the local aquarium store, and tropical fish magazines soon lay on top of the magazines devoted to my earlier enthusiasms: Field and Steam, Boy's Life, and Marvel comics. Eventually, motorcycle and body building mags would top the stack. Later magazines of pictorial interest could be found beneath a loose floorboard, for some reason.

I loved watching my guppies, black mollies, angel fish and gouramis in their ceaseless search for God knows what. This enchantment had its limits, however. When it came time to go on our annual summer vacation, I was faced with the dilemma of how to keep them fed for the two weeks that we would be gone. This was before the invention of timed, automatic feeders. Or at least my awareness of them. And we didn't have a sympathetic neighbor willing to take on the task. It appeared to my young and foolish brain that I had no choice other than to spare them a lingering death by giving them a quick one, via a dip in isopropyl alcohol. It's a decision that bothers me to this day. The fish deserved better. This shameful act was at the root of my reluctance to get another pet of any kind. I had been a bad steward once, and did not want to be so again.

Growing up in Palo Alto, my future partner and perpetual better half, Katie, had endured something similar. (I can't really call myself her soulmate because I lack another pair of legs and a tail). Katie, too, was not allowed a dog, even though she only had one brother and the nearby fields were covered with grasses. She was allowed a mammal, however; a gentle gerbil (is there any other kind?) named Wilhelmina. Katie had to promise that she would take care of her new pet; feed it, play with it, clean out its cage, etc. This was the easiest promise in the world to make, for a child living in the Present Moment, the only time that exists. And this promise she kept. For a while.

Then one day, as Katie was watching an episode of the Waltons in which a cow died, she got a sudden premonition that she had to go and check on Wilhelmina right away. She raced to her room only to make the sad discovery that Wilhelmina was no longer with us. The possibility that not having been fed for two weeks may have had something to do with it could not be discounted. Katie was heartbroken. The guilt and sorrow she felt as a result has accompanied her throughout her life, and still exists as a scab on her soul today. It is why, for a long time, she never wanted to be responsible for another creature again. Like me, she had blown it.

Much as we regretted it, Katie and I shared a common history of abject failure as pet owners. Bonding over shame is a dicey proposition, at best. But then, a couple years after we first met, we got a chance to make amends, to set things straight. It came in the form of a friendly, older, orange tabby named Eleanor.

We were living at the time in a rental near the border of Berkeley and Oakland. The converted house we occupied and a rear building formed a little compound of at least four apartments. Renters came and went over the years. The only permanent residents were Harry, the owner who lived in the back, and Eleanor, a scruffy, battle-worn orange tabby. She ruled the backyard, and lived with whichever lucky dweller she deemed worthy of adopting her. In return, she kept the precincts rodent-free and graciously allowed folks to pet her.

When Katie and I moved in, after duly checking us out—our habits, temperaments, scents—Eleanor apparently decided we would make do as her new humans and began insinuating herself into our lives. This, despite the fact that we had taken to calling her Norski; an indignity. Her adoption of us happened by degrees. I don't quite recall how she moved indoors with us. Only that one night, while I was fast asleep, I felt something suddenly land on my back… something with claws. I instinctively whirled up, probably screaming, and Norski didn't so much fly as scrabble through the air, landing on the other side of the room. After realizing what had happened, I, of course, had to make my apologies to Norski, who kindly took that to mean she was welcome to move in with us. And she was.

She was a lovely cat, and we grew very attached her. But she was older and sicker than we realized. We took her to the vet when she fell ill and discovered that perhaps "Norski" was a good name for her after all, as "Eleanor" was a he, not a she. What we don't know about animals could fill volumes.

Sadly, Norski got sicker and sicker, and in the end, we had to put him down. I took him to the vet's. Katie stayed home; she couldn't have handled being there. I was upset at what had to be done, but took some comfort knowing it was the right thing to do at the right time. What really affected me that day was seeing a young man sitting on the threshold outside the office, crying openly and shamelessly. His errand had been the same as mine, although his loss was obviously more deeply felt. Seeing him, I thought…those are beautiful tears.

Norski was a bright spot in our lives at that time. In allowing us to care for him, he helped heal and redeem our childhood sins against our former pets. Our relations with the animal world had resumed, and we had lived up to our roles as stewards.

Eventually, it was our turn to move out of the compound. Katie's parents had grown up in New York and New Jersey, which contributed to her life-long fascination with the East Coast. Katie decided it was the Promised Land. California's beautiful landscapes, kind weather, and open-minded citizens paled in comparison to Philadelphia's urban sprawl, cruel winters, and tribal communities, and so move we did. Eastward Ho!

We settled in an apartment near the University of Pennsylvania. I started a painting contracting business.

Katie got clerical temp work while continuing to produce portfolios full of her autobiographical, colorful artwork. After a couple years of me being the only verified animal in the household, Katie began dropping hints that it might be nice if we got a cat. They were low-maintenance, and besides, there were so many of them in our neighborhood in need of rescue. It was heartbreaking. Wasn't it?

Well, yes. Of course it was. Still, I wasn't thrilled with the notion. The ghosts of the murdered mollies still swam somewhere in my psyche, and I felt a reluctance to take on the responsibility for caring for another life, Norski notwithstanding. It seemed we had our hands full just trying to take care of ourselves. We weren't exactly thriving, financially. Still, a crack of receptivity opened in my cold acorn of a heart.

Then one day, strolling downtown, we passed the office of a local veterinarian. Frolicking felines regularly graced its storefront windows, with the result that they were often voted Best Peep Show in the City. We always stopped to check out the latest stars. Sure enough, several adorable kitties were slumbering in a pile on the cat bed. Good thing they were sleeping; any more cuteness and we might have had to enter the office right then and there and risk adoption. I took it as a small victory that we didn't.

When we got home, Katie opened up her astro calendar, closed her eyes, plopped down a finger on the page, and announced that on this date, there would be an orange tabby kitten up for adoption in the display window of the Cat Vet and that it would be ours. Not only that; the kitten would be 6 weeks old, making it a Taurus. To this day, I have my doubts that the Zodiac has any applicability to species other than our own. And even then I have my doubts. But that's me.

Katie, on the other hand, is a true believer. Not surprising for someone with five planets in Taurus. Or so I'm told. It supposedly explains her acute sense of smell and taste. Being an earth sign, it is also why she feels an affinity to the earth and animals. She is certainly more in tune with their needs and wants than I am.

Still, I don't think even she knew why she made this prediction, just as she didn't really know why she had to return to the bistro that night. I said okay, sounds good, but inwardly chuckled and promptly forgot all about it. This was the middle of February, after all, and the date she pointed out was June 15. What were the odds?

Months later, the day came, and we happened to be having coffee at a cafe near the veterinary office. I had forgotten all about the prediction, although Katie, of course, had not. While I paid the bill, Katie ran ahead of me to look in the window. It was with a sinking feeling that I watched her face light up with excitement. Lying on a cat bed, looking at us as if wondering what took us so long, was the orange kitten soon to be known as Boofy. Resistance was futile. With a prophecy fulfilled, who could argue that he wasn't divinely ordained to become part of our lives?

Well, I could, for one. But it did me no good. Into our small, second-story, one-bedroom apartment, crammed with books and the usual clutter of yard-sale junkies, came Boofy and his litter box. It was an adjustment for the both of us, at first. We doting on him; him doting on himself. But as time passed, the heartstrings that were initially tugged eventually became firmly wrapped around this special creature, who became ever more dear to us the more he seemed to take us for granted. I began to assume that every cat possessed this character defect of thankless detachment.

That is, until Dali, Hugo, and Blackie joined our tribe. All cats in need of a home. Dali, picked off the side of the bustling freeway she had just miraculously crossed. Blackie, abandoned in our neighborhood. Hugo, given to us from a household that could no longer endure the charms of his indiscriminate spraying. Again, you open the door to one, and before you know it you're buying Friskies by the crate and litter in 55 gallon drums.

All of our cats had their own quirks and personalities. Boofy loved to act the retriever by going after sipping straws we tossed and bring them back to us time and again. The phrase "pulling a Boofy" entered our lexicon, referring to anyone grasping at straws. He seemed pretty aloof to us, but the other cats loved him and took turns nestling near him and grooming him to within an inch of his nine lives.

Dali, aka "Pudgerella Waddlebutt," was a fat, orange and white tabby cat with black button eyes who thought every feeding might be her last, a complaint made in a kitten's high-pitched mew despite her massive size. The fact that her belly dragged on the floor didn't prevent her from leaping onto the bed, often with a roll of toilet paper in her mouth to offer me as a present. One day we came home to find a roll on my pillow, with a straw neatly perched across it. And to think I questioned their gratitude. Dali took a special liking to me, which she expressed by regular lickings of my skull and generally depositing a sticky layer of smelly drool wherever she saw exposed flesh. I wouldn't have minded a little less love from her.

Blackie , aka "the Silent Muncher," was the largest, most powerful of the cats, but also the gentlest. Unless some poor vet tech tried to minister to him, that is. Then he became a savage panther, and only I or Katie could calm him down. He was a loner, and often seemed sad. But when content, he had the greatest purr.

Blackie is a pretty uninspired name for a black cat. That's because we only knew him first as the wandering pet of our student neighbors, and that's how we referred to him when we saw him. Then the students left in the middle of the winter, abandoning him, and we found him hiding in an old garage. We took Blackie in. And he was forever grateful. Although not, perhaps, that we never changed his name.

And then came Hugo, aka "God's Gift to Earth." The star. Katie's true soul mate. A good description of Hugo would be…Pure Love. Disguised as a smushy-faced mix of Blue Lynx Point and Siamese (we think). He was grey, well-proportioned, with a bulbous head and large, round, blue, "alien" eyes. Think Gollum. We sometimes called him "Smeagy," after Smeagol, Gollum's predecessor.

Hugo was the sweetest animal you could imagine —equally loving to humans, fellow cats, and even other species. (Maybe not mice). The day Hugo left this world was a very dark one indeed, for Katie. His remains reside in an ornamental urn in a place of honor in our house. We still have a hairbrush with some of his fur in it. Katie swears that as soon as she has an extra $50,000, she will have him cloned.

I long for the day that proposition might be tested.

All of our cats expressed affection and gratitude towards us, their rescuers. And we were happy to have them. Each was clearly content with the new surroundings in our apartment, and, thankfully, with each other. No cat fights that I can remember.

At a certain point, Katie and I moved from our crowded apartment to a slightly more spacious two-bedroom, two-story row home in the suburbs. Much like the miracle of the loaves and fishes, the clutter that had occupied every square inch of the old apartment now seemed to have multiplied and done the same in the new place, making us feel right at home. In no time, every square inch of wall space in every room was covered with the artwork I had been collecting for years. Friends who visited named our house "the mini-Barnes," referring to the unusual way artwork was displayed at the Barnes Foundation in Philadelphia. We half-thought of charging admission.

The cats took to their new surroundings right away, and before long they each had their own roost in which to enjoy their being undisturbed. The stairs were a novelty, and gave them some extra exercise. There were occasional periods of chaos, as rooms got re-modeled and improvements were made. But the regular rhythms of life soon returned, and the successful co-habitation of the species continued.

I thought that having four felines who all got along and who were more or less grateful and loving towards us would have plugged that hole in Katie's heart that wanted a furry friend. Especially when one of them was Hugo. Together, I thought that he and I would have been enough for her.

I thought wrong. Hugo and I weren't enough. Hugo, Blackie, Dali and Boofy and me weren't enough. Katie's heart still required one thing more. And it would change our lives.

CHAPTER TWO

"Oh, Michael, Michael! Do you see them? Oh my
God, they are just the cutest things ever!!"

I saw them all right, and was doing my best to
give them a wide berth. Unsuccessfully. Up ahead, on
the sidewalk in front of our local cafe where we were
headed that winter morning, were two admittedly adorable Pomeranians lounging at the feet of their owner.
Chubby, sporting almost bouffant fur hairdos adorned
with pink bows, these pooches were shooting doggie
grins at every passer-by, practically begging to be petted.
Katie was only too happy to oblige.

"Michael! Look at these guys! Can you believe it?
These are just the cutest, *cutest* dogs in the world!"

Yeah, I looked at those guys. And yes, they were undeniably extremely cute. But I couldn't believe they were
the cutest dogs in the world. That's because Katie said
the exact same thing only yesterday about the Dachs-
hund puppy she came across on her weekly pilgrimage
to the local thrift store to search for vintage fabrics. And

I seemed to recall the same compliment being paid the week before that to a Jack Russell named Hank that belonged to a neighbor. They couldn't *all* be the cutest dog in the world. What gives?

When I brought that inconvenient truth to Katie's attention, she shot me that special, scornful look she reserved for when I was being even more exasperating than usual.

"You know what I mean. Why do you have to be such an OMG?"

The world might be interested to know that the acronym OMG existed long before its popularity on the Internet, Facebook, Instagram or Twitter. And it did not originally mean what it means today. I'd like to be able to say it meant "Oh, Michael Guerin." Or, perhaps, "Overtly Masculine Gentleman." For some unknown reason, Katie decided that it should stand for "Old Man Grumpus," an appellation I disagreed with while often living up to. Like now, apparently.

"Yes, I know, Katie. I know. Dogs are the cutest things. But you know we've got our hands full with our four cats. And a dog would need even more room and care! How could we do that? You know I'm right. Right?" This came out a touch feebly.

Katie didn't say anything, but shot me another look which as much as said "we'll see about that, buster." She stood and hitched up her Big Smith overalls, tossed her mane of brown hair, adjusted her hand-tooled hippie-era leather bag, and went into the cafe and ordered a coffee.

Her reactions were not a surprise to me. I had begun to sense something in the air for a good while now; a stirring, a wrinkle in the psychic space that comprised our relationship life. Katie was up to something. There were smiles, looks, and then asides and outright comments. And, disturbingly, they all revolved around canines. How they were the cutest animals on the planet. The same planet that hosts Panda cubs and Koala bears, no less.

This was not a good sign. It could only mean one thing. But I didn't want to face it. I am a master of denial, if I'm anything. I could make this go away. *Why yes, how unbelievable...that was the cutest dog I've ever seen! By the way, what did you think of that movie last night?* My powers of mis-direction had never failed me before. I was sure they could counter-act this new, hopefully temporary influence canines seemed to be having over Katie. No matter that pooches were starting to appear on our computer screen, in our mail, and amongst our refrigerator magnets. So what if the Dog Whisperer was showing up a lot more often on our television screen? I was the Katie Whisperer! It would just be a matter of time. This was just a passing fancy. Plus, we had absolutely no room for another animal. Anyone could see that. With my two best friends, Logic and Reason, I was convinced I would have no trouble talking Katie down from her mania to get a dog, should the question ever come up.

I was wrong. To her credit, she let me down easy, using my own strengths against me. *Why no, I wasn't really thinking of bringing a dog into our house! We don't have any room! At least, not for a big dog. A small one, maybe. Anyway, I just like to look around and see what's out there.*

What she meant by that was that she was already looking online at the shelters offering dogs for adoption. This, she knew, was my Achilles' Heel. I was a sucker for an animal in need. Besides our own four cats, I had rescued many others over the years, with most of them ending up in happy homes. Much of my contracting work takes place in neighborhoods where folks have trouble providing adequate care for their own children, much less having the funds to spay and neuter their pets. Consequently, the streets are filled with cats leading a rough life, especially during the icy winters. I cannot just leave an animal to suffer if I can do something about it.

I tended to name them for the streets where I found them. There was Ludlow, Hazel, Washington and Walton. Fifty-seventh and Woodland had to settle for Woody. I would take them to the vet's, keep them quarantined for a while, and then return them healthy enough to be presented for adoption. Not everyone made it. A couple had to be put down. But it was always worth it. I think if people were to extend their understanding of the Golden Rule—to treat others as you would want to be treated—to animals, even just a little, the world would be a better place. Especially for the animals.

What I didn't know was that Katie's online search for a dog had been going on for some time, and with some specificity. This wasn't just browsing. There was a goal in mind; a Holy Grail of caged canines. The specs were all down on paper. Unbeknownst to me, Katie had been writing letters to the universe for years, and putting them in a wooden box which had previously housed expensive chocolates. You might call it extreme visualization, made manifest. Her request to the gods was specific: she wanted a young Chihuahua, female, housebroken, fixed, healthy, and of pleasant disposition.

But writing letters to the universe wasn't the only metaphysical effort she made to find the doggie of her dreams. Some years ago, Katie found herself the recipient of a free, round-trip airplane ticket and decided to visit the city that haunted her dreams, New Orleans. She had a blast, especially enjoying the Voodoo Museum and the New Orleans Ghost Tour. But it was at the St. Louis Cemetery that she really sealed the deal as far as pre-ordaining her future pet was concerned.

This was the cemetery where the famed voodoo priestess, Marie Leveau, was entombed. Legend has it that if you bring a gift to her grave, you will be granted a wish. Katie dove deep in her handbag and laid some red-and-white striped peppermint candy before her grave. Closing her eyes, she prayed with the intensity of the true believer, beseeching Madame Marie for the same boon she had requested in writing from the universe. "Please bring me a Chihuahua, please bring me a Chihuahua…"

I didn't know about any of these efforts. Which was probably good. The more in the dark, the better. My resistance was futile, anyway. With the Universe and Madame Leveau on her side, how could I win? There was really only one additional stipulation that had to be there if I was going to get on board with Katie as far as this doggie thing was concerned. That was that the dog we were to adopt must be living on borrowed time. A beautiful picture of the perfect candidate would move me not a whit if it happened to be posted on the site of a no-kill shelter. She knew what my reply would be; that we really can't afford to take another pet on, and besides, someone else better suited to care for it was sure to come along sooner or later. There would be absolutely no pressure for me to do anything about it.

Of course, the same could not be said for the sites of the organizations that processed large numbers of lost, abused, unwanted, and rescued animals. By sad necessity, each creature has a limited time in which to try and attract an owner—a shelf-life span, so to speak—before they have to be put down. And although every single one of them deserves to be adopted, and almost every variety of cats and dogs are represented, that special Chihuahua that existed in Katie's heart apparently did not exist in the gallery of future adoptees for a long time.

And then, one day, it did. I don't know which day it was because I, of course, was still in the dark. Apparently, Katie had been in contact with a particular organization for some time, and had described exactly the kind of dog she wanted, instructing them to contact her should such a fated creature arrive on their doorstep. Arrive it did, and the email was sent out. Katie checked out the photo, liked what she saw, and began the delicate process of breaking the news to me about this future new resident in our house, and of melding my will to hers.

As with all successful brainwashing efforts, it happened by degrees. Conversations about the pitiful plight of stray dogs, during which I unsuspectingly voiced my complete sympathies, then turned towards the existential. And the confrontational. What was our moral duty towards these poor creatures? Put more plainly, what the heck was I going to do about it? With my guard now up, I spluttered what I thought was an acceptable reply as to why, in general, we had already lived up to that particular duty and were therefore absolved from further obligations.

Katie had no use for things "in general." It was too late for that. Things were now specific and personal. This wasn't a hypothetical castaway somewhere waiting for me to solve a metaphysical riddle. This was ZeeZee! Katie's detailed vision made manifest. A small, jet-black, personable, female pure-bred Chihuahua patiently sitting in a cell an hour's drive away, even as the clock that measured the extent of her existence was winding down. The situation brought to mind some advice I once heard and filed away, just in case I was ever kidnapped and held hostage. I should try and make the captors see me as an individual; with family, friends, and a unique identity, as opposed to being a "captive." Similarly, I was no longer dealing now with an abstraction. I was dealing with ZeeZee. And Katie.

And yet still I protested. I wasn't going down without a fight. In a final, perhaps kind effort to again let me down easy, Katie said that she wasn't a hundred percent sure she could handle another animal, and she didn't know how our cats would react to a dog, and, yes, our place was so small, etc., etc. It made me feel as if my arguments had gotten some respect and gained some rapport.

Then she dropped the bomb. She was going to drive out to the shelter the next morning. Oh no, she wasn't going to come back with anything! She was just going out there *to see the dog*. That's all. Just wanted to see her in person.

Even I, Master Denier, could see through this canard. This was a placebo proclamation if there ever was one. It was meant to be taken at face value, offering a little false comfort, whereas in reality I knew that once those two pairs of eyes met, that would be it. Done deal. Of course, Katie knew that too, but she put it out there in hopes it might temporarily soften my opposition and offer her some cover at the same time. I couldn't stop her anyway. If she wanted to waste some gas going to see an animal we would never own, who was I to stop her?

The next morning, Katie was waiting outside the shelter's doors an hour before they opened, dressed in her special vintage striped overalls; the ones with images of smiling dogs scattered all over it. When the staff arrived, they let her in and took her to the area where the strays were kept. She faced a long corridor, on the right of which were the cyclone fence enclosures housing the suddenly alert population of loud and lonely dogs. She slowly began walking the gauntlet, lovingly acknowledging the beseeching occupants as she went, but only for a moment, not wanting to offer false hope. There was only one dog that really existed for her as she proceeded down the hall. The others were mere phantoms.

The way Katie describes her first meeting with ZeeZee brings to mind a scene from the movie "Silence of the Lambs." CIA agent Clarice Starling is walking past a host of caged psychopaths en route to her first interview with the brilliant but insane professor and infamous human flesh foodie, Hannibal Lecter. As he comes into her view, she is startled to find that he is standing at still, perfect attention; his intellect and senses already completely focussed on her presence. The rest is cinematic history. Spoiler alert: thankfully for Clarice, she was apparently not kosher. Others were not so lucky.

To say ZeeZee stood perfectly still would be an exaggeration; there was some wiggling and waggling, I believe. But she was completely concentrated on Katie. She sat in that supplicating canine posture, with three paws firmly on the ground and the fourth held up as if waiting to be shaken. And although Zees may have intuited, in her doggy brain, that some sort of interview was going to be had, she was silent. No whimpering here. Too proud to beg. Her most surprising aspect, however, were her ears. ZeeZee has bat ears. That's what we call them. Spread out, they look like Bela Lugosi going out for a spin. And they were in full glory that day: completely extended to form a silhouette that was almost reptilian.

After a few minutes of soul-staring, Katie went back to the office and asked if she could hold ZeeZee. They took her to a room that was empty except for a chair in the middle. And then they let ZeeZee in. She took a moment to dissect the molecules in the air, sniffing and huffing like a junkie on a jag. Then she ran a couple laps around the room, and, without further ado, launched herself onto Katie's lap and proceeded to attack her face with her tongue as if she were made of pate and bacon. All without uttering a sound. (Ah, the good old days). As Katie soaked in the love, along with the saliva, she knew immediately that this was going to be her dog. At long last, her totem, the animal spirit that had haunted her dreams and been trotting around ethereally in her heart for a long, long, time had been made flesh and was pressing against hers with an insistence that was both pleading and persuasive. The die was cast. Now, how to tell Michael.

That really wasn't a question that caused Katie much struggle. How to tell me? I think it went something like "I'm getting the dog." Declared with a finality that made any possible objection sound like the depraved whimpering of a soulless sub-human. I was beaten and I knew it. I knew it the moment she said she was going up just to see it. Katie knew it too, and in a sportswoman-like gesture, did not come home with ZeeZee on that same day. She spared me that. She told the disappointed and dis-believing clerk at the shelter that she had to talk about it with the person she lived with, but that she would come back in a day or two. After all, it would be good if I were included, and anyway there were some preparations that needed to be made. Katie's plan was to return in a couple of days, adopt ZeeZee, bring her to a vet to get checked out, just in case, and then go home.

My plan was to stay out of her way. And, hopefully, the dog's as well. Bowing to the inevitable did not mean I had to embrace it. Even though I had never owned a dog before, I knew some of what was sure to be in store. Walks, feedings, nail clippings, walks, grooming, visits to the vet, teeth cleaning, walks, poop scooping, baths, walks, walks, and more walks. I glimpsed a future in which all of these tasks would make my present, already time-poor life seem like the epitome of idleness. It was a future I wanted to avoid.

And I almost did. Because when Katie called ahead two days later to arrange the pick-up (after sapping me of my free will and resistance), the clerk said that ZeeZee was being "interviewed" at that very moment by a couple interested in adopting her. If it went well, then we would be out of luck. She said to call back in an hour.

The minutes ticked by. There was a lot of praying going on. Katie praying for one outcome; me for another. Katie made the call, and again, just like when she saw our kitten Boofy in the display window, the look on her face told me everything. To say that Katie wears her heart on her sleeve is like saying the sun is hot. Her heart is worn not just on her sleeve, but on her shirt, sweater, coat, hat, hair, and on her aura extending five feet in every direction. She exploded with joy. She grabbed the bag of clothes and toys she had purchased for ZeeZee, collected our cat carrying case, and tore out the door.

In the office, they brought ZeeZee in as Katie was signing the papers. That was when our future canine princess decided to voice her approval by treating Katie to the rapid succession of ear-piercing, high-pitched manic barks that we would later come to realize was her default method of communicating with us and the world in general. ZeeZee's earlier, Zen-like silence was just a ruse; a wily strategy to win humans over. Her real nature is a combination of nervousness, aggression, and rabid anti-socialism. Once she gets to know someone over time, whether human or animal, she will show her sweet side. Until then, her modus operandi is to treat every creature in our vicinity as if they were on the verge of separating our souls from our bodies with a paring knife. Two year-old toddler or four hundred pound sumo wrestler; it makes no difference. As far as ZeeZee is concerned, they're all out to get us.

None of the things Katie brought for ZeeZee ended up fitting her, but it didn't matter; just as long as she fit into the carrying case. On the long ride home, she was perfectly quiet, which we later realized was an exception to her usual rule of whimpering and whining piteously whenever traveling by car. Could it be that anything—even being abducted by a stranger, put in a box, and careening towards an unknown fate—was preferable to the caged and lonely life she had been living at the shelter? Could ZeeZee possibly have intuited that she had been rescued just in the nick of time? Are dogs and cats smart enough to understand that not all of their fellow cellmates that come and go end up in better surroundings? That some never receive human visitors, yet get taken away anyway, and don't return? Whatever their thought processes, no one who has witnessed a dog's ecstatic joy upon being released from captivity can doubt that it counts among the greatest experiences that creature will ever have.

We have wondered at times if ZeeZee's crying while traveling in a car might be because she thinks we're going to bring her back to the shelter. And that would not be an irrational fear, because ZeeZee had been dropped off there before by her previous owners. We don't know who they were, how long they had her, or why they felt that they had to give her up (although I had a clue once I got to know ZeeZee's personality). All we know is that at the tender age of one, she had been torn from her home and deposited at the shelter, at which time a clock immediately started counting down the two weeks worth of minutes left for her to live.

We did find out that her name originally was Ani. Maybe Ani's transition to her new home and owners might have been made easier if we hadn't changed her name. But we weren't crazy about Ani. And Katie wanted this to be a new start; for us and the dog. ZeeZee is the name she came up with. We had both known a lovely and energetic mongrel called ViVi, which we were told meant "Life" in Hebrew. It sounded good, but was already taken, so Katie modified it to ZeeZee. Actually, ZeeZee Zelenka. I wasn't really crazy about this name either, initially, but it grew on me.

I was sitting on the couch when the two came in the door. Katie unzipped the case, and, out, torpedo-like, shot a compact, jet-black banshee of a dog, with spindly legs and impossibly large ears. She stood stock-still, looking at me; her nose working overtime. I guess I passed inspection, because she didn't bother to growl or bark. Once she determined I was of no obvious conse-quence, an estimation with which I am distressingly fa-miliar, she started exploring the Strange New World that was to be her home for the rest of her life. And although our house is small, it's filled floor to ceiling and wall to wall with all manner of niches and objects begging to be sniffed, so her inspection took a while.

And, of course! There were the four cats to contend with. I didn't take any sort of precautions with them in anticipation of ZeeZee's arrival. I figured they'd all have to manage to co-exist somehow, so why put it off? The sooner they got to know one another, the better. I don't remember where any of them were when ZeeZee en-tered, but I was certain that eight other eyeballs besides mine were checking her out at that exact moment.

And then ZeeZee did something that surprised me, shattering a long-held conception I had about the dynamic between cats and dogs. She utterly ignored them. Oh, maybe in passing she gave them a quick sniff and turn of the head, but, like me, it was apparent that cats were of no real consequence. It is an attitude she has maintained to this day. On a walk, ZeeZee will usually start barking as soon as she sees or smells another dog or a person nearby. But she could come face to face with a cat and not grant it the attention she would give an old shoe. Which is to say, she gets along with them. Who knew? Not me.

As ZeeZee went about exploring, Katie asked me the Question: "So, what do you think of her?" I have spent many years trying to make amends for my reply. "Well, she looks kinda ugly, don't you think?" Katie's mouth dropped open and she looked at me as if I had just confessed to matricide. When, when, will I ever learn this lesson? When your better half asks your opinion on something, and you already know how he/she feels about it, one should never, NEVER, allow honesty to interfere with agreeing with her/him completely.

It's not that I thought that ZeeZee was actually ugly. It's just that I didn't think she looked like how pure-bred Chihuahuas typically look. She is large of frame, bigger than most of her breed. Being solidly black was also an uncommon feature. And the fact that she had a "deer" shaped head as opposed to an "apple" shaped one, which is the norm for Chihuahuas, made her even stranger-looking. She was definitely a breed apart from her breed.

But so what? Who cared if she would never medal at the Westminster Dog Show? It would take me a while to realize that there is no more beautiful creature than the one who loves you unconditionally. I repeat: unconditional love for ME, the most imperfect of men. A guy who may have nothing more to offer the animal kingdom other than my unique scent. Someone that even relatively few humans have taken a shine to. And yet, she came to love me without reservation. That is what made my "ugly" comment shameful. True beauty is not just skin or fur deep; it is what lies beneath. And by that measure, ZeeZee is truly the Mona Lisa of mammals.

After an hour or so of apologizing for my ignorant comment, I settled into my new life with a new species. We introduced ZeeZee to our enclosed, postage-stamp sized backyard, notable only for its wide variety of weeds and the fact that it is bounded on both sides by properties occupied by certifiable nut-jobs. On the left was the hoarder. When she was finally evicted, work crews spent several days taking truck loads of garbage out of her house. That explained the odors that had seeped through our party walls over the years. ZeeZee, setting a good example, ignored her.

On the right was the hard-luck family of vampires on drugs. Never seen during the day; lights on in the house all night. They contributed a different, chemical smell to our household, thanks to "leaving the pan on the stove" on a regular basis. They did love dogs, however, as evidenced by the old bread and garbage they threw in our back yard from time to time, "for the little pooch." Hard as it was, ZeeZee managed to ignore them as well. If only we could do the same.

Back inside, Katie made the decision that ZeeZee was not to go down into the basement. Ever. Which, in a small, two bedroom, two story row house, is really cutting down on available territory. But the cats' litter boxes were kept down there, and Katie felt that they should have their privacy while doing their business. Plus, the cellar basically consists of two narrow, walkable lanes amidst towering walls of ill-gotten booty acquired thanks to a nasty addiction to yard, moving, and flea market sales. One man's trash may be another man's treasure, but it often just becomes another man's trash as well. Best that ZeeZee avoid it. The closest Zees has gotten to the basement is to poke her head past the doorway on the landing and look down, just checking to see if I'm okay while doing that always dangerous chore, the laundry. Her ever-present concern for me is palpable. More on that later.

Somehow, the cats, the dog, and we humans navigated through the new channels that had opened up in our relationships and made it to night time. Time for bed. Which raised a question we hadn't thought of until then. Where was ZeeZee going to sleep? We hadn't yet bought a dog bed for her. We knew nothing about her sleeping habits. Was she a sofa kind of gal? Would she hide? Did she snore? Would she sleep through the night? We were clueless.

Drawing on my vast experience with sleeping canines, I told Katie not to worry; the animals would figure it out. We went to bed, turned out the light, and lay there staring into the darkness.

There was the sound of a commotion. And what may have been a feline screaming bloody murder. Katie yelled out my name and turned on the light, just in time to see our new cannonball of a Chihuahua in mid-air vaulting onto our bed. She landed and immediately started tunneling down beneath the sheets, coming to rest at our feet. There might have been a sigh. There definitely was the sinking of a paw nail into my calf. And with no more ado, ZeeZee claimed her bed space as if we had always been saving it just for her. We might get in her way from time to time, but, always the under-standing canine, she will gently nudge us to the far sides of the bed with her paws, where we belong. More than anyone, she is a firm believer in the adage "let sleeping dogs lie." The humans can fend for themselves.

And so our lives began anew. Something really did feel different. Even though we had lived for a long time with our four cats and loved them all dearly, ZeeZee's presence and attentions were an experience of animal love on a whole new level. We assumed the cats all loved us. We had to assume, as they keep such feelings so close to the vest. But, we were to find out, there is no need to assume with ZeeZee. She can't contain her love, and doesn't care if the whole world knows it. Over time, being the recipient of such unending and uncon-ditional affection starts to make one feel worthy of such love, deserving even. Once you start accepting this love, you can't help but feel better; about yourself, and life in general. And that, indeed, is to live life anew.

ZeeZee had been with us now for ten hours.

CHAPTER THREE

Ever since ZeeZee bounced into our household, life can be divided into B.C. and A.C.; Before Chihuahua and After. The before part is starting to become a bit hazy. What could we possibly have been doing with our time when we didn't have to walk our little princess multiple times a day, or stop everything to let her out into the backyard when she wanted, or been busy concocting a cuisine which would suit her fancy?

By contrast, our four cats prospered practically hands-free. They had litter boxes, and they knew how to use them. Meals were always the same and served at the same time, with no complaints. They didn't really need to go on walks; their nocturnal prowling seemed to provide all the exercise they cared for. And, thanks to their surfeit of self-esteem, our cats didn't feel the need to pester us to pet them, or to cry out regularly for acknowledgment of some kind. They already felt pretty good about themselves, and we could only envy their self-possession.

And ZeeZee? Well, there's no getting around it; she's needy. The breed is known to often be high-strung, and in that regard, she does not disappoint. We all have to deal with our genetic inheritances. Take me, for example. With a highly introverted, intellectual father, and an artistically-gifted mother, I sometimes feel like the left and right sides of my brain are forever at war. Katie is a wondrous amalgam of a distant, mathematician father, and a rebellious, artistic mother, making her a distant rebel. These emotional inheritances were gifts for which we were not always entirely grateful.

ZeeZee is no different. She is the epitome of all the quirky, feisty, and out-sized personality traits to which the breed is heir. Chihuahuas have been described as being courageous, lively, proud, adventurous, sassy, cheerful, and agile, among other things. ZeeZee is all of those things. I would add ornery. And clingy. But that's only because she favored me, as I was soon to learn.

Perhaps a description of her behavior during a typical walk can serve as an illustration. At first, everything seems normal. Stops at the local fire hydrants to inspect their most recent baptisms: check. Obsessive nasal vacuuming over invisible points of interest on the sidewalk: check. Turning around and looking at us to make sure we knew she was the cutest thing ever: check. And then she would go over to the dark side. The second she would see or smell one of her own species, her own little Chihuahua Kundalini would migrate to her most base, combative doggie chakra. In the right light, you could see the hairs on her hide rise up in a diamond pattern, like a Gothic Mohawk.

And then the Barking would commence. It is a Primordial Yawp, blasting through and past humans' puny auditory sensibilities into the mysterious, alien eardrums of her fellow canines. Judging by their response, her barks were probably the doggie version of some choice four-letter words. It doesn't matter what kind of dog she might encounter; a full-grown German Shepard or majestic Great Dane would still get an earful. Our mailman fared no better.

ZeeZee doesn't seem to get that size matters, and there have been many times when we have had to scoop her up in our arms so as to insure her safe passage past a cadre of canines she had just insulted. Humans usually don't fare much better. The more someone bends down and attempts to sweet-talk her, the more she rewards them with incessant barking and snarls. Ignore her, and she'll invade your personal space in a heartbeat. The girl can't help it. She's man's best frenemy.

But inappropriate barking is not her only virtue. Inappropriate licking is another. The thing about ZeeZee is, she only displays animosity towards strangers. Once she gets to know you, everything changes. The growls stop, and she quickly develops an interest in ex-foliating every square inch of your available epidermis and reaming out both of your nostrils via her over-active tongue. These extreme expressions of love are not for everyone, and we have plenty of neighbors content to remain distant acquaintances of ZeeZee.

Being unfamiliar with the breed, we didn't realize until too late that she wasn't going to be another Lassie. The friendliness that we had always associated with dog behavior underwent a severe re-appraisal. Now, with ZeeZee and her attitude, we finally understood that every other human in the world is out to get us and is guilty until proven innocent. Guilty of what, we didn't know, but apparently ZeeZee did. I can't describe what a relief it has been to know that, while on a walk, that eighty-five year old dowager seemingly just strolling by with her walker was actually a would-be assassin. Only a lunging, hysterically barking canine stood between us and a premature exit from this world. That's how she rolls.

Chihuahua's aggressiveness is probably a lingering defense mechanism from the early days of the breed. They emerged from the area of the state in Mexico that bears the same name, and were prized in both the Toltec and Aztec civilizations. If a Chihuahua was lucky enough to belong to a royal household, it was treated like a god of the animal kingdom. Until, that is, it would be sacrificed to some other, higher god. Chihuahuas roaming amongst the general populace didn't fare much better. If one crossed the field of vision of an Aztec citizen, what came to mind was not so much "pet!" as "dinner!" So there may have been many good reasons why a little ferocity became a breed characteristic. What they lack in size they make up for in sass.

Experts rate Chihuahuas among the top ten watch-dogs. That describes Zees, all right. During the day, her guard is constantly up. No child, senior citizen, or neighbor is spared her suspicion and animosity. At a certain point in the evening, however, it seems she clocks out. We learned this one night when a police officer knocked on our door with his heavy-duty flashlight way past midnight. It had to do with some commotion next door. To be awakened out of a deep sleep by a pounding on our door certainly gave me and Katie a start. We had no idea what was going on. And until we did, going downstairs and answering the door was a bit scary.

Not for ZeeZee, however. That's because she stayed sacked out on our bed, not stirring in the least. As soon as any after-hours crisis or kerfuffle arose, ZeeZee's formerly sharp senses would desert her and she became blind and deaf in the face of the provocation. Perhaps it was her self-preservation instinct at work. Nothing bad could happen as long as she kept on sleeping. Once the sun went down, she punched out. She had finished her shift, loving and protecting us and driving us a little crazy. We were on our own until dawn. 'Til then, we were the guardians and Zees the guardee. Again, that's how she rolls.

As the weeks passed, and then months, another disturbing aspect of the Chihuahua breed began to come to light. And again, because we hadn't troubled ourselves to read up on it, it came as a surprise. It seems Chihuahuas tend to bond with one person. And slowly, scarily, it became more and more apparent that that one person was me. Katie, the human being who followed her heart

45

and sought out just that particular type of dog, rescuing her from certain death and doting on her every minute of her waking and sleeping life…well, she was just okay. This despite the fact that Katie lavished love on Zees in every way possible; buying her all kinds of matching outfits, photographing her incessantly, and then even using those pictures to create a series of paintings immortalizing her.

Katie is a graduate of the prestigious San Francisco Art Institute, which may come as a surprise to those who knew her as a child. That's because she didn't exhibit any interest in drawing or painting for quite some time. An art teacher in high school told her that her work was horrible and that she had no talent. But something happened a short while later. Almost overnight, a torrent of creativity burst forth via any nearby pencil, pen, brush, crayon, marker, you name it. Katie couldn't leave a blank surface alone. She took her work to the Dean of Admissions of the Institute to see if she might be able to take some classes there in the future and was accepted on the spot.

Katie has sold her bold, colorful work on the Internet, and has also written and illustrated two children's books. The painting which best expresses her feelings and devotion to ZeeZee bears the revealing title "My Dog Is Way Cuter Than Your Baby." It was included in an exhibition showcasing work by local artists in our area. It's safe to say it was among the more controversial pieces presented. At least to the new parents in the crowd.

ZeeZee seemed to take all this attention from Katie for granted. Once she had seduced Katie into rescuing her from the shelter, Zees endured her affections with an air of resigned tolerance. But me? The heedless lunkhead who never wanted a dog, who complained bitterly every time my presence was required on a walk, and who gave her the paltriest petting possible? Well, I was It. The Greatest Person to Walk the Earth. A man whose scent—a killer combination of paint thinner, chardonnay, and subliminal alienation—was obviously nose candy to any canine worth its salt, and especially to ZeeZee.

Speaking of nose candy and scents, I have to say a few words here about ZeeZee's olfactory prowess. It defies belief. She is certainly not alone amongst canines as far as this superpower is concerned, but, being relatively new to the dog world, it was a revelation to me. Zees could smell a ghost's fart a hundred yards away. While I go outside in the morning to see what the weather is like, she goes out to smell what it's like. When she stops on a dime during a walk and her nose vibrates, I'll have no idea what's going on until a block later, when an obviously evil Brussels Griffon rounds the corner and Zees gives her a piece of her mind. I sometimes lose patience with ZeeZee when I let her out in the backyard to answer Nature's call, only to have to wait a couple minutes while she just stands there, sniffing. Little do I know, she *is* answering Nature's call; processing scentual data from days ago and blocks away.

I've often wondered what living in this world would be like if my own sense of smell was as extraordinarily sharp as hers. Would it be a blessing, or a curse? There's no way of knowing. But, being a human, I tend to think it would be a curse. I guess I think there are more unpleasant smells out there than nice ones. But I doubt very much it is a belief that ZeeZee would share. Any dog owner who has witnessed the avid interest their pooch has in other pooch's poop knows that there isn't much their noses find objectionable. And I really shouldn't judge it. A dog's sense of smell can become so finely attuned to a human's physiology that low blood sugar levels in diabetics and incipient seizures in epileptics can be detected. They can know when something's off in you before you have a clue. They can track and find a creature who is lost, as well as one who is about to become dinner. The world of smells is their own private universe. We're just standing on the sidelines.

Since we're on the subject, just a word or two about ZeeZee's own smell. I will not do it justice, as my own sense of smell is not one hundredth of hers. But, if pressed, I would have to say that after sniffing around her ears and fur, and especially around those apexes of aroma, her armpits, the thing she smells like most is a neglected freshwater aquarium, one with real plants. Kind of a soggy, mossy, fetid scent… even more pleasant than it sounds! And with perhaps a hint of rancid popcorn. Maybe her aroma would change if we gave her a bath one of these years, but so far, that's been her signature perfume. Why mess with Mother Nature?

I'm not sure if my scent had anything to do with ZeeZee's obsession with me, but obsessed she was. Her realization of my greatness grew over time, but really surfaced full-bore several years ago when I became suddenly and mysteriously ill. I'm not sure what did it. It was probably food poisoning, which I had experienced before, unfortunately. But I also recall shaking hands with a guy in the street that day, and smelling an intensely penetrating, almost painfully aromatic cologne on him, which stayed in my sinuses for at least twenty-four hours. Regardless of origin, I started to feel queasy, then sick to my stomach. Soon, its contents began their spastic journey back up from whence they came and into the calming waters of the commode.

I was violently sick for twenty-four hours. I managed some sort of nightmarish sleep the first day, only to wake up to continued vomiting. Katie, who tried to do everything she could to ease my suffering, said that I looked like a broken street light, my complexion alternating between yellow and green. I had never before experienced any illness that debilitating. I felt helpless, defeated, and weak. The depletion of my system was so great that I lost much of my sense of balance for the next several days. Katie had to accompany me and hold my arm so as to steady me when I had to go about taking care of my business.

ZeeZee was with me every moment of my agony. When I lay on my bed, recuperating from horrific bouts in the bathroom, she tenderly licked my face and snuggled as close to me as she could get. When I had to get up again, she would accompany me to the bathroom and stand solicitously by my side through the retching and the stench, and then accompany me as I wobbled my way back to the bedroom. Once I again fell prostrate on the bed, the licking resumed, as if it was a required antiseptic response to the vomiting.

No one has had a more diligent nurse. Through the fog of my illness, I began to feel the kind of consolation, love, and healing a pet can offer a human. I was too sick to feel appreciation for much of anything, except her. Never under-estimate the restorative power of another heart beating right next to yours, especially ones cloaked in fur.

After many days, I eventually returned to my normal state of health. But something was different. It used to be that only my shadow followed me. Now it had company. Zees would not leave me alone. Whether I was answering the doorbell, the phone, or Nature's call, it didn't matter; they were no longer solo activities. It's as if she didn't trust that I could take care of myself. What else could explain me getting so sick? My well-being became her concern from then on. And she's been doing a pretty good job of watching over me. I've never gotten that ill again.

She has, though. Despite our diligence in trying to make sure that nothing strange gets in her mouth while on our walks, one day ZeeZee ate something bad. Poisonous, even. Later that day, on our front lawn, she started convulsing, and from her mouth streamed an alarming amount of a nasty, yellow, custard-like substance. She then fell onto her back, lifted her legs into the air, and became motionless; her eyes open but blank. And she stayed that way.

This happened when I was at work. Katie was with ZeeZee, and practically went into convulsions herself when she saw what was happening. Katie fearfully bent down and touched ZeeZee's side, to see if she was still alive. Zees responded by instantly whipping around and biting her finger, drawing blood. Biting was something that had never happened before. Katie swept her into her arms, and somehow managed the challenging task of driving our flailing dog to the vet's office without me there to help. ZeeZee was put on medications, and eventually recovered. I tried to be with her as much as possible. I doubt that my presence helped Zees as much as her presence helped me, but I know that our mutual illnesses and care-giving brought us even closer together.

Even though she knew it was silly, Katie sometimes felt jealous and hurt that I was the Chosen One in ZeeZee's life. Before she rescued her, Katie had a whole, idyllic future mapped out in her imagination for herself and her dog-to-be. They would dote on each other, and snuggle at night and whenever snuggles were needed. They would delight little children, and old folks, too. They would take rides in the car together, going to flea markets and parks and other cool places, soul sisters of different species.

House, yard, and moving sales had figured prominently in the lives of Katie and me for some time

now. We loved the thrill of the hunt for cool and unusual items. It was a drive which eventually led me to
collect works of art by and of African-Americans wherever I could find them in the neighborhoods in which I
worked. Amazing treasures could be found languishing
in dusty corners in even the most dilapidated of storefronts. Over time, I eventually assembled a collection
that illustrates the tremendous creative energy of the
descendants of the African Diaspora. And they were
hiding in plain sight. Who knew?

But could Katie take ZeeZee on any of these sojourns? Turned out, no way. Traveling in a car with
ZeeZee is an exercise in stress and frustration, for her
and us. She hates it… crying, barking, whining and
whimpering non-stop every second of the trip. The out-
ing every other canine seems to love terrifies her. Whatever happened to that attribute of "courage" Chihuahuas
are purported to possess? It flies out the window once
she enters a car, along with her howls.

Even if Zees somehow made it to a block sale, she'd
be quite a handful, defending me from those creeps who
were obviously out to get me. And forget about letting
little kids try to pet her; they would need all of their fingers later on in life, after all. Sometimes ZeeZee allowed
Katie to cuddle with her, but was happier being cuddled
by me. So things hadn't worked out exactly as Katie had
envisioned. Hardly at all, in fact. She still loved ZeeZee,
with all of her heart. And Zees loved her, with half of
her heart. It's just that Katie wished that she would have
been the Chosen One. Many times, I wished it as well.

It was only many years after we got ZeeZee that I learned why she acted the way she did; why she was so confrontational to canines, people, and creatures in general. Zees obviously suffered from "Small Dog Syndrome." It describes a set of behaviors that can occur when owners of small dogs treat them like babies instead of disciplining them just as they would a larger dog. It can actually be stressful for a Chihuahua to be treated like a baby; what they really need to feel is that their owner is strong-minded and capable of handling an entire pack of pooches. If that mastery isn't sensed, then a small dog might just decide to fill the vacuum and elect itself the pack leader, the Alpha Dog. As such, it will exhibit jealousy and aggression with other dogs, snap at children, be suspicious of every human except their owner, and generally be on edge a lot of the time. That's our Zees, all right.

Much of this imprinting can take place during the puppy years. Whatever other interactions ZeeZee's previous owner may have had with her, treating her just as one would a larger dog wasn't one of them. It was clear…she had been babied. And now she thought she was the Leader of our Pack. Hence, her protectiveness.

I wasn't insulted. No one in any group or clique to which I belonged ever mistook me for the Alpha Male. I'm solidly in the Delta or Epsilon corners. And it's endearing, in a way, to be the recipient of ZeeZee's obsessive attentions; I won't deny it. It might be co-dependent, but I'm no stranger to that dynamic. Anyway, the die was cast. ZeeZee is the way she is, and I love her both because of and despite her attitude, if that's possible.

Over time, Katie, me, and our boss, Zees, became a pretty solid pack. We were tight. If any one of us suffered a misfortune, the other two were there to console. The Wheel of Fortune brought us ups and downs, but being a threesome made it an easier ride. While I once couldn't imagine life with a dog, now I couldn't imagine life without one. It was a different world.

The years passed quickly, as life ruled by routines often does. One by one, our beloved cats exhausted their nine lives and went on to meet their Maker. The inky-black young dog that Katie rescued from the shelter became grayer, as did I. Zees and I both put on a little weight. And despite me having a huge head start in the aging department, we were both middle-aged.

ZeeZee wore her years more easily than me. She still seemed just as fast, curious and nimble as she was when she was just a year old. What had changed was that Katie and I were now, undeniably, her family. She completely trusted us. She relied on us for food and shelter, and we relied on her for love and affection. Talk about a bargain. Giving relatively little, we got so much back in return. Our household was filled with that particular undercurrent of joy and happiness that only those lucky humans with loving pets enjoy. We assumed it would always be there, as long as she lived.

We were wrong.

CHAPTER FOUR

Katie and I have not taken many extended vacations together. There was the trip to Hawaii that Katie won in a radio contest many years ago, before ZeeZee came into our lives. We lived the high life for three nights at the beautiful Waikaloa Hilton, then extended the trip on our own dime, staying a few more nights at a cheap motel down the road that barely managed hot water. The two cats we had at the time were left in good hands.

For a couple years, we were treated to a few nights stay at a magnificent lake-side Victorian resort in up-state New York, courtesy of Katie's aunt. It was gorgeous and relaxing, our peace of mind aided by knowing our by then four felines were again in good hands.

But ever since ZeeZee arrived, taking vacations together for any protracted length of time became a thing of the past. We just hadn't found anyone or anyplace that we felt was capable of handling ZeeZee's personality and behavior for more than a day or two at a time. And so we fell into a pattern where one of us would go off for a few or several days while the other stayed home and took care of the menagerie.

The longest time I was away was the week I spent in Spain, attending a wedding and visiting my many cousins there. As soon as I left, ZeeZee fell into a deep depression and was inconsolable the entire time I was gone. She stationed herself by the front window and door, waiting expectantly until it was time to go to bed, when she would ever so slowly hoist herself up the stairs, climb unto the bed, and plop herself down on my pillow, where she would spend the night. She was devastated, and putting up with her wasn't much fun for Katie, either. I returned home to a hero's welcome from ZeeZee, a zero's welcome from Kate.

This arrangement of one of us taking off while the other dog-sits was getting old. We needed more from a vacation than just that. We could really use an extended time away from our usual routines, when we could decompress in some beautiful new surrounding. Hawaii was many years ago. We were due.

But there was another reason why we felt the need to get away. Katie and I, for a long while, had been drifting apart. The currents were slow, but steady. The trouble with opposites attracting each other is…well, we're just so darn different! In so many ways!

Katie is a planner; she investigates things and takes initiative. The calendar is her friend. I acquiesce, your typical leaf in the wind. She'll want to discuss upcoming plans with me regularly, and I will regularly try to put such talk off indefinitely. It exasperates her.

Katie is a worrier. I joke that she can't really be happy unless she's worrying about something. I, on the other hand, tend to think things will always work out. Katie expresses her out-sized emotions without a filter; she lets it all hang out. Emotions rarely get past my filter. When it comes to being in touch with one's feelings and honestly communicating them, I'm an emotional midget and she a giant.

Katie leans towards the Obsessive/Compulsive operating system. When she gets into something, she *really* gets into it. And she is effusive in sharing her passions with others. I tend to subscribe more to the "Que Sera, Sera" school of thought: Whatever Will Be, Will Be. It camouflages my laziness, a bit.

The worrier part of Katie, combined with the compulsive part, means she's always checking to see if things are locked: car doors, house doors, windows, phones. The door-to-door salesman is really casing the joint. The neighbor's active fire pit will likely burn the block down. The smell next door comes from a meth lab. There is no end of reasons to be fearful. I prefer to think things are okay. Even when I forget to lock the door(s).

It all comes down to mountains and molehills. In my world, there are a whole lot of molehills, relatively few mountains. In Katie's world, there's not much difference between them. If you were to transcribe everything Katie says in a typical day, seventy-five percent of the sentences would end in an exclamation point. My speech pattern might feature five percent. The resemblance to my parent's disparate temperaments wasn't lost on me. I guess history was repeating itself.

When life throws one of its many curveballs at us, I have more trouble dealing with Katie's reaction to it than with the problem itself. And when something major appears and I treat it like it's no big deal, it drives Katie crazy. It's a fail-safe recipe for mutual exasperation.

A perfect example of how much my laissez-faire attitude could infuriate Katie, while at the same time illustrating how much she cared for me, came when she saved my life. This is true. She did. That happened a few years after I saved her life. This is true. I did.

The first event came about when Katie started to have an allergic reaction to a bad combination of foods. In an effort to control it, she took some medication made in Canada which she had purchased online. We waited for it to take effect.

It took effect, all right…it made things worse. Katie's face started breaking out in lumpy red patches. Her lips started ballooning and her eyes started disappearing behind the flesh puffing up around them. She looked like she had just gone nine rounds in the ring against a superior opponent.

Despite that, she wasn't eager to go to the hospital. Maybe she was worried about the possible costs. Or thought the swelling would go away on its own. Unfortunately, neither of us was familiar then with the phenomenon of anaphylactic shock. We had just never run across it. But it was happening right in front of us.

In the middle of the night, I said that's it, we're going to the hospital. Katie didn't resist. When she went to the admitting window, before she even said anything, the woman behind it looked at her with widening eyes and asked "do you always look like this?" Katie shook her head. That was the signal for a couple orderlies to throw her on a gurney and whisk her away.

It was a close call. If we hadn't gone to the hospital when we did, her throat would have started closing up her airway. We were foolish not to have gone earlier. Katie is never now without her EpiPen.

A few years later, I started experiencing shortness of breath when going about ordinary activities. I had to stop halfway up a hill to catch my breath. Climbing the stairs left me in the same boat. These episodes started increasing in frequency, usually instigated by some sort of aerobic activity.

Like any Stoic worth his salt, I chose to keep these anatomical events to myself. I didn't want to alarm Katie. Plus, if I could only just ignore and deny these bothersome symptoms long enough, surely they would go away on their own, wouldn't they?

Not a chance. While I was away from Katie for a few days, visiting my siblings who were vacationing at the beach, the episodes became so frequent that I checked myself into a local hospital. Although the staff was unable to replicate my symptoms or diagnose my illness, the attending physician urged me to go home and see my doctor right away. That very evening, after describing what I had been going through, my doctor looked at me a little strangely and said that if he were me, he would check himself into a hospital right away. That got through to me. And that's what I did.

Of course, this was all news to Katie; a shocking, extremely belated disclosure that had her beside herself with anger. The secret I had kept out of some misguided sense of consideration was rightfully seen by Katie as an example of how I wasn't open, honest, or sharing about what was really going on in my life. She is an open book; she holds nothing back. I had just held something very important back, and it made her mad as hell. Her anger rose to an even higher boiling point when I managed to make matters even worse. That's when she saved me.

After staying overnight at the hospital, I was given a stress test on the treadmill. Sure enough, the reaction was triggered; my heart started beating four times its normal rate. The cardiologist was sitting at a table doing some paper work, not paying attention. The nurses looked at the screen, then at each other, and then grabbed the doctor. He saw the monitor display, and, like a pro-bowl fullback, tackled me and laid me out on a table. He clamped his hand around my throat and started throttling me. This, apparently, was a way to abate the reaction.

I was diagnosed with RVTO—right ventricular tachycardia. Basically, an arrhythmia set off by the adrenalin caused by exertion. It is a condition which, if left untreated, is why young athletes might collapse and expire on a basketball court. Our own cat veterinarian met his end due to the same condition while also exercising on a treadmill. The solution, for me, was to have an outpatient surgical procedure. I made an appointment to have it done in two days time and went home. I was advised to take it easy.

The next day, doing a little research, I discovered that the hospital I had chosen was not amongst the providers that my insurance company covered. Getting the procedure done there would cost me thousands of dollars more than if done in a hospital covered by my plan. No problem. I did more research, cancelled my operation scheduled for the next day, and arranged for it to take place in a hospital included in my plan's providers. Problem solved! Only hiccup…the operation couldn't take place for at least three weeks.

I made this decision unilaterally. Again, without consulting Katie. And again, when she found out, the Furies were unleashed. What was I thinking? How could I have not informed her about my choices? And why was I risking my life to save a few bucks? What was I… crazy?

Well, if you put it like that, then…yes…I was crazy. Katie helped me see that. Thanks to her piling on, I did the right thing and re-scheduled the operation to take place the next day at the original hospital, no matter the extra cost. I was spared three weeks of walking on eggshells, tempting Fate. Who knows what might have happened?

Katie cared deeply for me, no doubt. But she was also driven crazy by me, by my stubborn resistance to completely opening up and being emotionally honest with her. I hold back. It doesn't make for a healthy relationship. A widening gap which was increasingly hard to bridge had opened up between us. We were having a lot of trouble finding the fabled Middle Way that the Buddha espoused. For each of us, it was getting more like my way or the highway. Not good.

And, of course, there was that traditional relationship bug-a-boo, money. Mutual funds. Trouble was, they weren't mutual. It was all on me. Katie tried, but her efforts rarely resulted in income sufficient to her needs. That was a problem. But just as vexing, for me, was how she set about trying to solve it. I would come home from work and ask her how did it go today? There was this thing called a newspaper, which posted a lot of help wanted ads back in the day. I assumed this was something she was checking.

Katie's enthusiastic answer was that she had just discovered some new book on manifestation or visualization, which, when mastered, was sure to bring about the desired financial outcome. It all starts on the Inside. Another answer would be "Great!" and then she would proceed to show me the beautiful illustration she had painted that day for her children's book in progress. Someday it would pay off.

I loved her paintings; they were wonderful! Nothing wrong with doing them. Not a problem, that is, if my last name was deMedici. But I doubt if Lorenzo's patronage stemmed from an income for two of fifteen dollars an hour. Michelangelo might have spent his whole life quarrying marble rather than carving it had that been the case.

Maybe our problems were all my fault from the very beginning. We started dating right after that first meeting at the bistro. Katie was sub-letting a room in a house in the Oakland suburbs at the time. We had a particularly magical experience outside that house one night, which seemed to augur well for our future relationship with felines. We were sitting in my car, talking and kissing into the wee hours of that misty night when we were startled by some noises. We looked up and were treated to the sight of some neighborhood cats coasting down the wet windshield on their bellies and then sliding further down the hood of the car before dropping out of sight. They then circled back, leapt onto the trunk, then the roof, and then slid down again, over and over.

We were astounded and delighted. It was as if we were bearing witness to a previously unknown aspect of feline behavior—the Secret Midnight Slippery Sedan Slide. We felt honored they had chosen us.

Things were less magical inside the house. Katie was in a difficult situation. Part of the sub-letting deal stipulated that she was to clean up the house in exchange for a reduced rate. That was the cue for the primary renters to embark on a new phase of party-giving and daily culinary experimentation. The kitchen was always a complete mess, as was the rest of the house. Katie was supposed to keep it immaculate. If the number of hours she worked to uphold her bargain were tallied, her room was very expensive, indeed. Even Cinderella didn't have it so bad.

Enter Prince Charming. Scratch that. Prince Charming would have been nice, but what she got was me. All I could offer was a temporary haven living with me. I was camped out at the time in what barely qualified as a shack, high in the Oakland Hills, and which was in the process of being sold through probate court. Settlement was only four or five weeks away. So our co-habitation would have a definite time-stamp on it, but at least it would be better for Katie than staying where she was.

But that's not what happened. Beware the Unexpected Development! Four weeks became four months, and, not surprisingly, we found ourselves in a very different emotional place. We were closer, but also more aware of our differences. Living together long-term so soon after meeting had not been our original intention. And now we wondered if continuing to do so was the right course. A decision had to be made. Our new agreement was that we would continue together in a new apartment until such time as Katie was able to get her own place.

That didn't happen either.

I had actually done the same exact thing in the earlier relationship I had after leaving the ashram. We had been together for a couple of years, although living apart, when the woman I was with had to suddenly vacate her house due to its sale and didn't have anywhere else to stay. I suggested we get a place together. It would make things easier.

It did make some things easier. It also made some things harder. Beware the Co-habitation of Convenience! We eventually arrived at a make it or break it point. Right on cue, a real Prince Charming did arrive, sweeping her away to the City of Lights. I was hurt, but it was the right thing. I was happy that she was happy. And although we didn't make it, we didn't break it either. We stayed friends.

How did I come by this faultless relationship wisdom and unerring judgment? I credit my ten years living in the ashram. It's not how most young folk spend the decade of their twenties. Instead of dating, "hooking up," and learning about relationships, I was delving into a completely different realm. And I'm a richer person for it. But it left me pretty far behind in the mating game. I was going to have to make a lot of mistakes in order to catch up. And to my credit, I did so with aplomb.

The funny thing is, despite our issues and differences, Katie and I could still have a great time enjoying life in each other's company. It was perplexing. Until, that is, I discovered the Key Principle which can solve any relationship difficulty. How is it therapists don't know this? Michael's Maxim Number One —"Once you give up on the Main Issues, the rest is a Piece of Cake."

When a nugget like that passes as wisdom, you know you're in trouble. We needed to sort things out. There is a song lyric that describes the place in which we found ourselves. It would have been nice if it was "love is a many-splendored thing." Unfortunately, it was more like "neither one of us wants to be the first to say good-bye." That's how iffy things had gotten. Since we had had so little success sorting things out on our home turf, we figured going somewhere new could only improve our chances. Hence, a vacation.

Katie had just the place in mind. Two summers before, she had gone by herself to Ocean Grove, New Jersey for a couple of days, and stayed at a quaint, beachfront hotel. People have been coming there to unwind and soak up the sun and sea for over a hundred and fifty years. It has been the destination of choice for various Christian denominations since Victorian times. The huge, beautiful temple at the town's center was featured in a Woody Allen film, and one definitely gets the sense of a by-gone era wandering the shady streets. There is a large encampment of permanent bungalows occupying a central square, which are family owned and have been passed down from one generation to the next through the years and which cannot be bought or sold.

I was describing Ocean Grove to a poker buddy, and mentioned that it was a dry town with a lot of senior citizens. He snorted in reply "sounds like hell." I guess heaven for him could be found just a short stroll up the boardwalk in Asbury Park, where the evil drink and, hopefully, loose ladies might linger. But if hobnobbing with gentle people in genteel surroundings suits your fancy, Ocean Grove is hard to beat.

We reserved a room for five nights at the same hotel Katie had stayed at before. I made arrangements with my contracting business so that things could still manage to limp along even without me. We stopped mail delivery for that week and packed our bags. The biggest consideration, of course, was what to do with ZeeZee. Taking her with us was out of the question. Even if the hotel allowed it, the two hour drive alone was enough to squash any notion of co-vacationing. ZeeZee's hatred of all things automotive had only increased with time, and our eardrums and nervous systems would not have survived the whimpering, whining, and wailing that was guaranteed to erupt in transit. A pet-sitter was the only solution.

Twice before in our life with ZeeZee, we had left her for two nights with a sitter we found through the Internet. I wasn't happy that it was a good fifteen minute drive to his house, but his rates and reviews were good, so we decided to use him.

On both of those previous occasions, things seemed to have gone smoothly. ZeeZee was, of course, ecstatic to see us again when we came to pick her up, and seemed none the worse for wear. Mitch, the sitter, even went so far as to say that he and his wife, Sonja, had grown quite fond of ZeeZee. That may have been laying it on a little too thick; Zees is not the most endearing of personalities. Regardless, I was happy to have her returned to me in good spirits. As far as I was concerned, leaving ZeeZee with Mitch again, although for almost a week this time, was fine.

It was not with Katie. Despite our having twice used his services successfully before, Katie nonetheless did not want to use him again. It was just a feeling she had. I couldn't understand it. What was the problem? We had used him before, twice, and gotten our dog back safe and sound. A + B = C, doesn't it? What reason could she possibly have to risk trying out a new provider when we already had one that we knew could do the job?

Well, reason had nothing to do with it. Her opposition had nothing to do with logic, and everything to do with a feeling deep within. Leaving ZeeZee with Mitch again just didn't "light up." There was no explaining it, it didn't make sense; it just didn't "light up." Period.

That should have been enough for me. Hadn't I had enough experiences witnessing the validity of Katie's intuitive flashes? Boofy and ZeeZee's presence in our lives alone were proof enough of that. Katie's getting a bad feeling? Case closed. No need to think further.

Except I did. My Inner Doubter, ably assisted by my Inner Lazy Bum, had to have its say. And Katie, bless her heart, listens to me. My voice counts, even if it says something with which she disagrees. I tried my best to convince Katie that it would be all right to leave ZeeZee with Mitch again. And I guess I was partially successful, because it delayed her researching any other suitable candidates until the vacation time was suddenly upon us and it was too late to make any other plans.

Katie wasn't happy about this. At all. It wasn't the first time I had countermanded her intuition. She accused me of being open to her connection to the world of inner feeling only when it suited me, and there was a lot of truth to that. It was my fault that we ran out of choices at the last minute. And so, on the morning of our first day of vacation, and with extreme prejudice on Katie's part, we seduced our little bundle of joy into entering the carrying case, and, ignoring her piteous baying, drove her over to "Uncle Mitch's."

Entering Mitch's house was a little like walking atop a pool table. That's because every square inch of the floor was covered with a hard, thin, hunter-green felt masquerading as a carpet. An impressive array of crystal decanters housing minimal quantities of variously colored liquids on a sideboard gave a hint that Happy Hour was not a time to be missed. From the dim bowels of the house came the yelping of an unknown number of captive canines.

We let ZeeZee out of the carrying case, and she immediately embarked on a nose-to-the-ground ex-ploration of this strange new territory. It was probably like going to Disneyland for her. Her aversions to travel and, basically, to all living creatures had made her a total homebody. The only other place Zees really went to was the vet's office, which was a lot different from this place. Her tail was wagging like a windshield wiper on the highest setting.

We sat down with Mitch and began going over the rather long list of details that he and his wife would need to implement if ZeeZee was to be nurtured in the manner to which she was accustomed. If nodding is any indication, Mitch seemed to take it all in, and afterwards started showing us a photo album of all the dogs they had boarded before.

That's when we witnessed the Harbinger of Things to come.

All of a sudden, Sonja burst into the room, gave Mitch a dirty look, jerked her head in the direction of the big picture window, and yelled "Outside!" before darting out the front door. Mitch leapt to his feet and ran after her. We looked at each other, and then out the window, just in time to see a fleecy white French poodle scamper from their front yard onto the street and race merrily down the dividing line towards God knows where. Behind her, much less merrily, lumbered Mitch and Sonja, shouting out "Whitey! Come here, Whitey!" They obviously got the name wrong, because this pooch was having none of it.

Katie and I ran out after them and joined in the chase. By sheer force of numbers, we managed to get Whitey more or less surrounded a block away. Katie instinctively sensed that a capturing-type vibe was not the way to approach this little runaway, and so switched to a more passive, quiet head space. Sure enough, Whitey ventured over to her as we were slowly boxing her in, and a few minutes later, was back where she belonged: behind bars.

"See what I mean? What did I tell you?" Katie whispered to me as we went back inside to find our own dog barking her head off, unsurprisingly. I could see the reproach and fear in her eyes. I didn't know what to say, so I said what I often say when I don't know what to say.

"It'll be all right; it's okay." Man, did I wish I believed it. "This was probably just a freak incident; I'm sure it doesn't happen often."

But how would I know? This might be a daily occurrence. Still, I wanted to be reassuring. Katie's look told me I was failing miserably. But there really wasn't much we could do about things at this late point; our vacation time was already ticking away. We were stuck.

Mitch came back into the room with a story about how Whitey was exceptionally smart and had figured out a way to undo the latch on the gate in the back yard. I wondered if he was referring to the combination lock I noticed there, in which case Whitey was not only a genius but extremely dexterous as well. Still, we gave him the benefit of the doubt and resumed going over ZeeZee's requirements.

Then it was time to say goodbye. We hugged ZeeZee and kissed her, but again, it was the opposite of reassuring. She whimpered and cried, squirmed and wiggled, and basically pulled every trick in the abandoned pet book in order to strike shame, guilt and sorrow into our souls. Unlike us, she succeeded. We straggled out the front door to the sidewalk, looking back frequently to see ZeeZee planted at the window, a black and grey, batwing-eared sentinel barking her brains out while shooting us pleading looks. We got in the car, wracked with guilt and already looking forward to the time when we would be picking her up and taking her back home with us.

It would just be six short days. But ZeeZee didn't know about time. In her mind, it was possible that she might never see us again.

In our minds, we thought we would see her again in a week.

One of us was wrong.

And it wasn't ZeeZee.

CHAPTER FIVE

Two and a half hours after leaving the sitter's house, we were cruising along the scenic oceanfront drive in downtown Ocean Grove, New Jersey. It was a brilliantly sunny day, with tolerable temperatures and gentle ocean breezes. It was noon, and since we couldn't check into our hotel until two o'clock, we strolled through the town, taking in the sights and dining al fresco at one of the many restaurants lining the main boulevard.

As we sat at our table, enjoying the sunlight, salad and sandwiches, taking in the parade of humanity who were, in turn, taking in us, I remember thinking…*man, a guy could really relax in a place like this.* Here it was, smack-dab in the middle of a Monday, a time when for decades I would almost assuredly be engaged in earning my bread by the sweat of my brow, and what was I doing? Cooling my heels, sipping a Sapporo at noon, and looking forward to a week more of similar indulgences. Without really wanting to admit it, I think we were both also enjoying that extra lightness of being that happens when a significant burden of responsibility is lifted. We loved ZeeZee. But we were more than happy to love her from afar, just for a little while.

Our hotel was a cozy, wooden Victorian gem facing the ocean and sporting porches and decks on each of its three floors. As we were checking in, I was already envisioning how delightful it would be to spend some time on the top floor, ocean-front balcony… settled in a rocker, watching the waves, and seeing the sun rise up from the sea the next morning. It was a great vision while it lasted, which was about five minutes. Turns out those ocean-view decks were available only to the occupants of certain, adjoining rooms. Our room, reached via a narrow back stairway, faced the mainland part of town. It did have a balcony, however, with a stunning, unobstructed view of a close-by stucco wall, and well within earshot of the metal trash dumpsters huddled below.

I guess that's called getting what you paid for.

But we didn't really care that much. Though it might be out of view, they couldn't take that ocean away from us. We could still smell it. And were itching to get into it. Even during the many summers when my vacation consisted of crashing on the couch of one of my sibling's rentals by the sea for maybe two and a half days, it all felt worth it if I could just get into the water. As soon as I was being smacked around by the cold waves, snorting a little brine, and getting a toe pinched by a crab, my real place in the universe was again brought home to me, almost on a cellular level. I'm just a creature. As needy and bestial as ZeeZee. Subject to the elements of Nature, and, unlike ZeeZee, of my own mind. And it just feels so good to bathe in one and escape the other. What were we waiting for? Get out that SPF 30!

"Do you think we should take our phones with us?" Katie asked. I knew she wanted to. Katie is a little too anxious to want to be all that disconnected from civilization, even on vacation.

"I don't think we need to" I replied. "Plus, they'll probably get sand in them and they might get ruined. Let's just leave them in the room; it'll be okay." There I went with that "being okay" stuff again. When will I learn?

But again, Katie listened to me. We went out onto the beach with a blanket, towels, and not much else. Our bathing suits, of course. This northern New Jersey beach was a bit different from the ones I was used to in the southern part of the state, but I delighted in the difference. Grittier sand, steeper drop-off. Same ocean, same realization.

Katie was hesitant to get in the water, even though she was suited up for it and we had come such a long way. I had gone in first, and tried to give her a little encouragement.

"Come on in, Kate! It's not that cold. Really feels good….you'll love it! Like taking a salt bath!" This was something she did at home. I'm not sure if salt baths were meant to ease one's body or one's soul, but I figured both could benefit from being in the ocean.

"Okay, I'm coming, I'm coming. Hold on."

I watched as she trudged hesitantly over the sand to the water's edge. Her weak left side could sometimes make navigating even on solid ground problematic. Keeping her balance on the shifting, uneven sand was much harder, and as I watched Katie approach, I felt appreciation rise up in me at her effort to do something which for others was so easy. It was, in essence, a small act of courage, although I was the only one on that beach aware of that fact.

Courage can take surprising forms. I obviously didn't have a lot of it when faced with a beautiful woman's eyes. And it isn't something Katie has in abundance of when faced with certain aspects of the physical world. Maybe it's because she has had such a rough time of it, right from the beginning, by virtue of her difficult birth. She came out of the womb face first, not like most of us. It was a bruising introduction to this vale of tears. She was diagnosed with scoliosis and cerebral palsy. Her entire left side suffered damage, from head to heel. Her left leg and foot are shorter than her right. She wore a metal brace from the age of two until five, cause enough for other children to throw stones at her and exclude her from games and sports while growing up in Palo Alto. To add insult to their injury, they treated her as if her physical disability meant she was also mentally deficient.

These are the sorts of experiences which leave scars. As if the invisible scars weren't enough, Katie's left forearm sports a large, smooth, darkened patch of skin resulting from the poor plastic surgery provided after she was run over and dragged by a car when she was nine.

Add to that a couple allergic and digestive sensitivities, and you have a woman who makes her way through this material world with a surfeit of caution.

But there may have been a silver lining. When Life taketh away, it also giveth. Katie has often wondered if the brain and body injuries incurred at birth were also responsible in some way for her extraordinary, highly developed sense of intuition. She must have gotten it from somewhere. I have witnessed her uncanny ability to accurately read people and events in ways that defy logic over and over again. It's like she possesses a super power, which she takes for granted and which I can only envy.

She is strong in ways many are weak. She's not afraid to speak her mind. (Sometimes, I wished she were). Most folks' number one fear—speaking in public—isn't a problem. I have seen Katie lead workshops in rooms full of strangers... informing, entertaining, answering questions, the whole nine yards. She displayed the same assurance when she managed a group of volunteers for an event with the Dalai Lama for several days. Driving in traffic can freak her out. Speaking her mind can freak other people out. She is nothing if not a study in contrasts.

Katie made it out to where I was bobbing chest high in the surf. She was smiling, although I could see she was also a little scared.

"Feels good, doesn't it?" I said.

"You know it does!" she admitted. She added; "Can I hold your hand?"

"Sure." The swelling of waves did nothing to help her equilibrium.

We enjoyed being suspended in the water for a few minutes, and then Katie revealed what was never far from her mind.

"Do you think ZeeZee's okay?"

My answer was tinged with a slight impatience. Why would she think Zees wasn't?

"Yeah, Katie, I'm sure she is. Why wouldn't she be? We left her in good hands. She'll be taken care of. You have to try and let go of your worries so you can enjoy being here. Otherwise, what's the point of even going away?"

"Okay, I guess you're right. I'll try."

I was glad to hear her say that. I myself hadn't thought of Zees since we put fifty miles between us and her. There was too much new stimuli to dwell on our sad leave-taking.

After marinating in the waves for a while, we stretched out on the blanket, drying in the sun and taking turns dozing. The people-watching was fun, too. That same parade of humanity we surveyed at lunch was marching by here, as well. The fact that we're all just creatures becomes even more clear when said creatures remove most of their clothes. I may have even espied a new species or two.

Before returning to our room, we decided to stroll on the boardwalk for a while. Going north, we came to a cavernous, aged structure built over the walkway. In its heyday, it must have housed a great many establishments. There were still a few businesses operating, but most of the space was sealed off. A giant mural of a busty mermaid with octopus tentacles rather than a tail lined one side of the building. A bit foreboding, I thought.

Exiting out the other side of the building, we discovered we were entering Asbury Park. An obvious difference from Ocean Grove became apparent when we saw the first of many outlets offering booze for sale right on the boards. Beer, wine, and even the demon rum were but a few feet and a ten spot away. Good to know. It was just possible that we (read "I") might need a respite from righteousness occasionally.

We talked about things as we walked along. Especially about what Katie had just been through a couple weeks ago. She has an elderly aunt who is a deaf-mute and who lives alone in an apartment in a less-than-ideal neighborhood in the Bronx. She suffered an allergic reaction to a failed vaccination as a child which resulted in the loss of her hearing. After attending a prestigious university for the deaf, she went on to a productive career working in medical labs.

But that was long ago. Her deafness had already caused her to live in a world of her own, and now that time and infirmity were pressing upon her, she was becoming even more isolated. It was only due to the kindness and help of a friend and fellow tenant—herself an active ninety-eight year old!—that Katie's aunt was able to get by. But a change and more help were desperately needed, so Katie went and stayed there for a week to see what she could do.

It was the most intense week of Katie's life up until then, resulting in something close to a nervous breakdown when she returned home. Everything had been difficult. She contacted and dealt with Social Services agents; accompanied her aunt to her doctor's office and a hospital; met with lawyers; had meetings with her aunt and her aunt's local banker; dealt with the negligent landlord; went shopping both with and for her aunt; cleaned her apartment; organized her papers; cooked, and generally did everything she could to better her aunt's situation. All while being exhausted. Sleeping on the worn couch was problematic, thanks to the din of the street sounds and the fact that her aunt could wake her up at any hour in order to tell her something. All communication happened by writing on sheets of tablet paper; her aunt had never learned to sign. It was often a frustrating interaction. Despite all Katie's efforts, her aunt resisted complying with the changes needed to improve her situation, and Katie returned home defeated.

And depleted. Completely. She suffered a Temporary Adjustment Disorder, characterized by depression, crying, feeling overwhelmed, difficulty sleeping, anxiety, feelings of helplessness, worry….it was bad. There's not a great buffer, no real protective barrier, between Katie and the slings and arrows of outrageous fortune. She feels everything deeply. This trip to the shore and the sea would hopefully help Katie recover from her ordeal, in addition to giving us a chance to sort things out. That was the hope, anyway.

And it seemed to be working. Both of our spirits were lifted by our new, bracing surroundings. We re-traced our steps and headed for the hotel, ready for a shower and then a seafood dinner later. But as we arrived at our door, we found a note taped to it, telling us to contact the front desk clerk ASAP.

Now there's a message we could have done without, especially on vacation. Still, we went into our room first, to get a bit more presentable. And we checked our phones. I looked over at Katie as she was listening to her messages, and watched as her large, expressive eyes widened in shock and her mouth dropped open. She turned to me, and with a voice cracking with horror, told me the last words I cared to hear.

"The pet sitter lost our dog!"

I just stood there; mentally repeating what Katie had just said and trying to make sense out of it. The pet sitter lost our dog. Our dog. ZeeZee. Gone. Lost. *LOST?* Where? Why? How? When? For some reason, it was just a statement I had great trouble getting my mind around. Because this really couldn't be happening. Our beloved, batwing-eared diva of a Chihuahua couldn't really be running around loose in this world, could she be?

She could. There were several messages left on our phones in the previous hours alerting us to that fact; messages we missed thanks to my wise decision to leave our phones in the room. So we were already hours behind when ZeeZee was actually lost. This was also difficult to compute. It's as if we were living in different worlds; Katie and I thrust into a new place with its own time, and ZeeZee also living in a new place, where time had no meaning.

Katie immediately called the sitter. Mitch answered and proceeded to describe how he had been taking ZeeZee out for a walk when she suddenly balked and not only clawed off the tight collar around her neck holding her license and ID, but also squirmed out of the halter we had given him and then took off running down the sidewalk. He tried to run after her, but 230 pounds of middle-aged flesh is no match for a Chihuahua/possible greyhound mix racing towards freedom. He gave up before his heart rate neared an active level, and returned home. Just as there are no atheists in foxholes, it was now obviously out of Mitch's hands and into God's. Certainly not Mitch's fault.

Katie was having a hard time believing that. And believing that ZeeZee could possibly have pulled off her collar with her identifying tags. It had always been a snug fit. To imagine that a) ZeeZee was possessed of an overwhelming urge to escape from it, and b) that she could have forced that narrow, tight band over her bulbous head and jaws, was simply unthinkable. And that she then extricated herself from the halter as well. Both of those things could not have happened. We were being lied to.

When Katie attempted to question what we were being told, Mitch became belligerent. "Don't you tell me she couldn't have done it! I was there! She escaped! It's not my fault!"

Katie had the phone on speaker mode. I could hear what he was saying, and his tone as well. For someone who had just failed in his paid, professional responsibility to maintain custody of a client's beloved pet, he certainly sounded the furthest thing from apologetic. In fact, he was angry. At what, I didn't know. At us? So it seemed. But I think he was angry at himself. He never once acknowledged that ZeeZee's disappearance had the least thing to do with his actions, and never once proffered anything close to a heart-felt apology for losing this creature that we were now, suddenly, and achingly, realizing meant the world to us. It was all her fault.

Katie hung up the phone and looked at me. We were both speechless. This really just couldn't be happening. It had been a beautiful afternoon, we were on our first day of vacation, we had made every preparation in order to a make this rare get-away possible, and now, suddenly, we were faced with the fact that a member of our household had gone missing. LOST! Nowhere to be found! And no one looking! The question of what to do hung, unspoken, for a moment or two in the stunned silence that marked our new-found reality. And then, without a third thought (okay, I might have had two), I knew what to do.

"I'm going back" I announced. " I'll drive there; you stay here. I'll probably find her as soon as I get to where she was lost. You know how she is."

By this I was referring to ZeeZee's unfathomable obsession with me. No matter what could have transpired to have caused her to flee from organized human society, I had no doubt that upon hearing the first syllable leaving my throat and entering her huge ears, she would make a dash for my arms. It was a sure thing. Then I could return her to the sitter, return to the shore, return to Katie, and return to the peace of mind only attained when one has done everything one's conscience requires. Simple.

Katie ended up agreeing with my plan, although it took a lot of convincing. She wanted to come with me and look for ZeeZee herself. That was the feeling she had. But I somehow made her believe that it would be better if I went and she stayed. She ended up saying okay, but only, I think, because we were both in a state of shock. Otherwise, I doubt she would have thrown in the towel.

We were both hoping that my confidence in finding ZeeZee right away was well-placed; neither of us was quite ready to give up on this rare vacation. While I returned to be the boots on the ground, Katie would be disseminating our info into the cybersphere. That was the plan.

I was also secretly praying that this arrangement of leaving Katie behind in anticipation of my quick return would have the effect of keeping her from falling back into the black hole of fear and anxiety from which she had only recently emerged. She was even more attached to Zees than I was. There was no telling how she might react if I didn't find Zees pronto.

I threw the clothes that I had just hours earlier stashed in the room's bureau back in my suitcase, ran down the stairs, jumped in the car, and some two hours later was parked in front of the dog sitter's house. I rang Mitch's doorbell and he let me in. Judging by the morsels adorning his T-shirt and the bulge in his jowls, it was dinnertime. Now, maybe it's just me, but if I had just lost a pet I was paid to look after, perhaps an apology would have been the first thing to come out of my mouth. Maybe it didn't from Mitch's due to the burger and fries already inhabiting it. And yet when he managed to swallow and speak intelligibly, he again started saying how it was all ZeeZee's fault that she was lost; that he wasn't to blame.

According to him, he was taking her out for her first walk when, only a half-block from his house, ZeeZee had suddenly balked and managed to worm her way out of both her ID collar and halter at the same time before racing away with a greyhound's speed till she was out of sight.

I wasn't buying this any more than Katie had earlier on the phone. For starters, ZeeZee's collar with all her tags was clipped snugly around her neck when we dropped her off. Without disengaging the locking mechanism, it would be physically impossible to force it over the bulb that was her head. And the halter, while fitting a bit more loosely over her frame, would have been a challenge as well, with its cross-binding design.

To escape from both at the same time and so quickly that the handler couldn't do anything to stop her? Houdini couldn't have managed it. So now, not only was our dog lost, but lost without her ID. She was micro-chipped, but who knew if that would ever be checked by whomsoever might find her? It was just more bad news.

But there wasn't time to argue. It was close to eight o'clock and I knew I had about an hour to search with light on my side. I pressed Mitch to tell me where ZeeZee had last been seen, and where he thought she may have headed. Before answering, Mitch decided that it was in my best interests to be made aware of the tactics recommended to find a lost dog, courtesy of a website that had just faxed him the info. I sat there, twitching impatiently on the edge of my seat, as Mitch slowly proceeded to read me the two pages worth of data, pausing dramatically before polysyllables before giving them his best shot.

It was unendurable. After a couple minutes, I leapt from my chair and said "Man, I gotta go!"

I jumped into my car and headed in the direction where Mitch had said ZeeZee disappeared. The entire neighborhood, for many blocks around, consisted of well-kept ranch homes developed in the sixties and sitting on good-sized tracts of land. The streets curled and looped in patterns that together enclosed a well-knit community of middle-class families. Surely there were many dog owners and dog lovers among them. I tried to keep that in mind as I slowly started cruising the streets, car windows down, and shouting out every ten yards or so a succession of salutations that ZeeZee would undoubtedly find irresistible.

"Here Zees! C'mere, girl! Come to Daddy!"

"Who's a good girl? ZeeZee's a good girl!

And the always reliable:

"Who wants turkey? *TURKEY ZEEZEE!*"

I felt a little uncomfortable hurling out these zingers towards people's homes. I had to get over something in me to be able to do it. Perhaps more than the average child, I had been raised to behave properly, to observe decorum. But there wasn't really any way to do that and at the same time do what I had to do to find ZeeZee. I would have to look the fool, at least according to my inner judge. And, just as in every other occasion in my life when I have had to transcend my inhibitions, the prospect was both scary and liberating.

I went for it, appearances be damned. Back and forth, up and down, further and further as the night descended, startling senior citizens, scaring kids, bedeviling dogs, and generally being a nuisance. But I didn't care. I had to do it. ZeeZee might be hiding just behind that garage. Or in those hedges. Or in the stand of trees just beyond that backyard fence. She could be anywhere.

But after searching for an hour or so with no response, my already heavy heart grew heavier still. ZeeZee was nowhere near, otherwise, she would have come to me. And if she wasn't in this neighborhood, then I was out of luck. The world extended equally expansively in every direction. Which one had she taken?

I had no idea. This was going to be a lot harder than I thought it would be when I was in Ocean Grove. Unlike what I had imagined, ZeeZee and I were still apart. There would be no re-union tonight. I admitted defeat and drove to our home, fifteen minutes away.

The house never felt emptier. Normally, every time I open the door to come in, ZeeZee is already there to greet me. A sniff and a lick, and then it's off to the sofa to bark for five minutes, celebrating this remarkable occasion which never gets old for her. Only after extensive petting will she tone down the decibels. Katie, on the other hand, could be gone all day, and yet when she comes home, ZeeZee, from atop her favorite perch on the sofa cushion, might at most give her a casual look as if to say "Oh, you again."

But that night, there was only silence. I unpacked the suitcase I had filled early that morning, and called Katie.

"You didn't find her, did you?" All Katie needed was to hear the sound of my voice when I greeted her. My tone said it all. Instead of jubilation, there was defeat.

I told her what had happened, and said I would be back out there looking first thing in the morning. She had spent the many hours since making phone calls and doing research on her phone and iPad. She contacted nearby animal shelters, left messages for the animal control officers of nearby towns, alerted our friends in the area, and posted messages on our Twitter and Facebook accounts. Through it all, Katie was somehow keeping it together. Which was amazing, considering how deeply she is moved by her emotions, and how terribly upsetting this news was. But she was being strong. Her intuition told her that's what was needed.

There was one more really incredible thing that Katie did that night. Or, more correctly, didn't do.

She didn't say "I told you so!" She could have. You can't say I didn't deserve it. Her dark premonition about using Mitch again had proven true, and her worst fears were realized, mainly thanks to me. Not only that; I was also to blame for not bringing our phones with us on the beach, against her wishes and thereby delaying our response. Also worthy of an "I told you so!" But she spared me that. And I appreciated it. A lot.

This was one of the things which had created distance between us... me favoring my rational approach to things over Katie's intuitive one. Which was strange, considering my own awareness of an inner world via meditation, and the countless times Katie's prescience had proven true. Perhaps I favored logic because my connection with my own psychic sense was so tenuous. But that didn't give me the right to disparage her remarkable gift, or dismiss it. Doing so created alienation. That was my fault. I was seeing that now.

I went to bed spent, yet unable to sleep; my mind ceaselessly playing out the events of the day and what might happen tomorrow. For once I had the whole bed to myself. And hated it. As much as I used to complain and harrumph at having to cede valuable bed space to ZeeZee, feeling her body next to mine was to feel loved, to feel one of the pack. The Alpha Dog, even. It was comforting on a bestial level. I'm a mammal, too!

I missed my shadow.

Katie's night was equally restless. She was trying to sleep in a strange bed in a strange room, alone in a town suddenly drained of charm. She would get up every so often to check or write something on the tablet, as ideas on how to proceed popped up. There were moments when the utter helplessness she felt threatened to over-whelm her, but she succeeded in escaping their grip. She couldn't afford to give in. There was too much at stake.

And ZeeZee? The nine pound alpha female of our pack? Our devoted, middle-aged, eternal child, who had last eaten at seven that morning, who was skittish of humans and mammals in general, and who had de-pended on us for her every need every day and night for the last eight years of her life—how was she faring? Had she eaten anything today besides her morning kibble? Was she sticking around the area where she had disap-peared, or was she still on the run towards God knows where? Was sleep even a possibility for her tonight, in her strange, bewildering new environment?

These were questions without answers. I felt frus-trated, defeated, and useless. The perfect mental cocktail to keep sleep at bay until the wee hours of the morning.

CHAPTER SIX

I woke up the next morning groggy and tired. Yesterday's drama was looping incessantly in my head and I felt more alone than I had for a long, long time. Many years ago, when I lived in California, I had a job in sales that had me traveling up and down the northern parts of the state, from Carmel to Arcata and the Sierras to the sea. Three or four days a week on the road was normal, yet I rarely felt lonely. It was a welcome respite from all the years I had spent living communally earlier in my life.

But that was before I was a member of a pack—me, Katie, and ZeeZee. Both Katie and I are comfortable with some time apart, and from being apart from ZeeZee, as long as she was in good hands. But as I lay there in the bed, feeling utterly isolated, I realized I had made another mistake: Katie should have returned with me. At some point, I'd have to make the several hours round-trip drive back to get her, losing valuable search time in the process.

My heart ached to have ZeeZee back by my side…
tucked under the blanket, tapping my tookus, being an-
noyingly adorable. The fact that she was somewhere out
loose in the world and I was powerless to help her was
utterly distressing. From a world where love and caring,
feeding and nurturing came from trusted hands, ZeeZee
had now been dropped into the eternal Darwinian
struggle for survival. Fight or flight. Prey or predator.

We had failed her.

The ringing of my cell phone snapped me out of my
funk.

"How'd you sleep?" This, at least, was normal. Katie
asked it every morning.

"Lousy. You?" I already knew the answer.

"Terrible. I was up most of the night on the computer. You've got to get some flyers made with ZeeZee's
picture on them and put them all over the streets
around Mitch's neighborhood. We've got to make people
aware of her, and do it soon. We need help."

She was right, of course. The more eyeballs, the
better. How wide an area might ZeeZee be covering by
now?

I said I would do it, but that first I would go back to
the same streets I cruised last night and see if I'd have
better luck. At this early point in a pet's disappearance,
without any reported sightings yet, one can only return
to the general vicinity where it was last seen and keep
looking.

"Katie? I know you're half out of your mind. But
hang in there. We've hardly begun looking for her. We'll

get her back. You've gotta know that; we're going to get her back." I was saying this for my benefit as much as hers.

"Yeah, I know. Okay. It'll happen." I detected some re-assurance in her tone, for which I was grateful. "Well, good luck out there."

"You, too."

"I love you, Michael."

I paused, taken aback. Those were words I had not heard in quite a while. Or uttered. The emotional distance that had gradually opened up between us had relegated our recent communications to the practical, the banal, and, too often, the testy. Sadly, we had gotten used to it.

I could picture the sincerity her beautiful eyes were undoubtedly displaying as she said this because I had seen it so many times before. Those words were always easier for her to say than for me. I can be witty, I can be facile, I can sometimes even make sense! But I have a hard time speaking my heart.

Katie doesn't. And when she says something she means it. And when what she says is that she loves me, it floors me some. Someone in this world loves me! It's the emotional equivalent of winning the lottery. Hearing her words stirred the realization that, despite all of our difficulties and frequent mutual exasperation, the feeling was mutual.

"I love you, too, Katie."

That wasn't so hard.

On the fifteen minute drive to the sitter's neighborhood, I began to bitterly regret that we had taken our dog so far away to be boarded. Chances are, if we had used the services of someone in our own little borough and ZeeZee had gotten loose, she probably would have been able to find her way home. We had gone on walks all over our little town. All she would have to do is sniff her way from fire hydrant, to lamp post, to telephone pole—in other words, the usual canine commodes—to trace her own spores back to our house. For a dog, all loads lead to Home.

As I approached where ZeeZee was last seen, I drove along a border of the East Course of the historic Merion Golf Club. Founded in 1896, it has consistently been rated as being among America's greatest golf courses, and has hosted five U.S. Opens. A second, West Course was developed in 1914. Both are meticulously maintained gems of engineered landscapes designed to bedevil even the most accomplished of duffers.

I noticed that the entrance to the West Course was within a quarter mile of where Mitch had said ZeeZee was headed. If she indeed made it onto the fairways, it could be a mixed blessing. There was plenty of water to be had at the numerous ponds and water hazards, which was a lucky break, this being late August. There was also a lot of open ground amidst the stands of trees, where even a speeding black dot like ZeeZee could be easily sighted. On the down side, I doubt that the club would allow the play of its upper-crust members to be disturbed by a madman running around the greens yelling "ZeeZee!" and "Turkey!" That sort of malarkey is reserved for the public courses.

Once again, I cruised the same streets of cookie-cutter ranchers I had surveyed last night, calling out for ZeeZee. There weren't too many folks out and about this early on a Tuesday morning, but those who were told me that they hadn't seen her. The dog-walkers, unsurprisingly, were the most sympathetic of all, and some said that they would go out looking for her later.

That blew my mind. Caring people, complete strangers to me, were now on board and offering to help. The fact that I was so surprised showed that I still had a lot to learn about people who loved dogs. For some of them, canines as a species place several notches higher than our own. News that some poor pooch was lost—anyone's pooch!—was a call to action. Little did I realize just how critical a role the kindness of strangers would play in the days ahead.

I decided to stop back at Mitch's house and touch base. He hadn't called me, so I didn't expect any news. But ZeeZee knew his house, knew there were other dogs there, knew there was food there, had probably pooped there, and might logically be expected to show up there again. I also wanted to see if Mitch had been doing anything to find her.

It's possible a 24 hour buffet operated in Mitch's household, as feeding was again in progress. In between munches, he filled me in. He told me he hadn't seen ZeeZee, that he had knocked on the doors of his nearby neighbors and given them a description, and that he was going to keep a sharp eye out for her when he was walking his other charges. That was it. All relayed in a fraternal tone as if we two should be commended for our selfless efforts in trying to find her, as if a dog so wild and stupid as to get herself lost barely even deserved rescuing. Not a hint of an apology. That ship had sailed. Today, he was a heroic volunteer.

That was about all I could take. I told Mitch that he should leaflet the entire area and continue looking every free moment he had. Despite what he would prefer the world to believe, he was the one responsible for ZeeZee's custody and the one guilty of letting her escape. I was holding him accountable. You couldn't blame the dog. She was only guilty of following her instincts, which understandably wanted to put as much distance between her and this odd-smelling stranger as possible. He was the professional charged with making sure that didn't happen. He failed. Open and shut case.

I went back to our house to design and print out a "lost pet" flyer. There were a lot of photos to choose from. Somehow, thanks to my almost utter cluelessness with all things digital, I only managed to print out a black and white image. But it wasn't a disaster. ZeeZee is all black and white and grey anyway. At least she was when we last saw her. Katie entertained fears that she might have turned completely white from fright by now, like the black cat that survived going over the Niagara Falls in a barrel with its owner, only to reputedly emerge an albino. But I had faith Zees looked pretty much the same. I added all the relevant descriptive and contact information to the flyer and headed off to Staples to make a bunch of copies.

Back in Ocean Grove, Katie had already been reaching out and spreading the news for hours via the Internet. After some time, she finally took a break and went out for a walk. It was a gorgeous day, warm and sunny. There was a religious service going on at the Kingdom Hall. She sat on a bench outside, near the doors which were all left wide open. She closed her eyes and joined in the prayers. It was peaceful there, silently petitioning along with the congregation; a welcome lull from the mental and emotional duress caused by ZeeZee's disappearance. She began to feel the deeper, still feelings within; those that always swell beneath our suffering. She could get through this.

But then the singing commenced. Out floated the strains of a hymn… "you're going to find Him, when you go to heaven…" And that was it. The floodgates opened. The staunchness and resolve which had accompanied her during the previous twenty four hours dissolved in gut-wrenching sobs and tears. Katie sat there, convulsing with a grief rising up from a deep place within she had never felt before. If absence makes the heart grow fonder, a disappearance makes it go berserk. The love she had always had for ZeeZee was now so painfully clear. Only when something that you take for granted has been suddenly taken away does its meaning in your life become obvious. Amidst her tears, Katie desperately prayed that it might be returned.

It must have been an arresting sight; this forlorn soul in colorful overalls crying her heart out alone on a bench while a gathering of the faithful sang to the Most High just a few yards away. No one stopped to ask how she was. Sometimes, though, that's okay. Sometimes people just need to be left alone. The storm passed. It was almost as if she had experienced a sort of emotional PTSD flashback of how she felt after visiting her aunt. But Katie knew she couldn't stay in that place. It was too debilitating. She collected herself and went back to the hotel room to contact more people. There was work to be done.

And that's when we got the First Call.

"I saw your dog!"

Those four simple words, uttered with a matter-of-fact certainty somehow more affecting than if they had been shouted, instantly turned Katie's depression into elation. ZeeZee was alive! Someone had seen her! Our prayers had been answered.

"Where? When did you see her?" Now Katie was shouting.

"I saw her yesterday; running down Ellis Road."

The woman's name was Meredith. She had learned of our plight from reading information Katie had posted on the County's lost Pet site. She had been driving home on the twisting and turning uphill climb that was Ellis Road, when, clearing a bend, she suddenly saw some kind of creature—she wasn't sure what—racing down the double yellow dividing lines of the street straight towards her car. She slammed on the brakes, stopped in the middle of the road, and got out of her vehicle. That's when she saw that the creature was a black and grey bat-eared banshee of a dog, speeding like a greyhound pursued by a panther.

Another car then came up behind Meredith's, and it, too, stopped in the road. The woman driver also exited her car, despite wearing what Meredith later claimed were pajamas. This lady saw ZeeZee running down as well. Both of them cried out to her, and tried to get her to come over to them, or to slow down, or to do anything other than commit the highway hari-kari our dog seemed hell-bent on executing.

ZeeZee zoomed by as if they weren't even there. What a surprise. Even in her normal state, on a walk with me, Zees would have greeted these two fine ladies with total indifference at best or a chorus of intimidating barks at worst. That's just her nature. But on this day? When her supposedly loving owners had taken her on a scary ride to a stranger's house and then left her there? For who knows how long or why? And when she had just heroically managed a harrowing escape and was fleeing towards anywhere but where she had been? Come over to strangers? You'd have better luck picking up a ball of mercury wearing a catcher's mitt.

Meredith started to apologize for not being able to grab ZeeZee, but Katie stopped her.

"No, please, we're just so happy that you tried, and for calling and letting us know you saw her. Now we know where she was heading. Thank you so much for trying!" Katie asked Meredith if she could call her again later, if need be. One never knows.

Indeed, this was progress. Without a sighting, our search could have continued indefinitely in the wrong directions. Now we knew where to focus our efforts.

But our luck wasn't over yet. A second call came in to Katie, this time from a woman named Edith. She, too, had seen our dog the day before, around the same time but a good bit farther away, at the intersection of Darby and Marple Roads. Now we had two areas in which to look. With me being the only one out there searching, that was about as much progress as we could handle at the moment. The two spots were a good mile apart, but if ZeeZee could cover the distance, so could I.

I drove over to the intersection where Edith had seen Zees. It wasn't a pretty sight. Oh, it would be if you were a motorist, speeding along the twisting asphalt and enjoying the dense foliage that came right up to the shoulder of the road.

But to me, treading on the meager ribbon of ragged asphalt that passed for a sidewalk and timing my sprints around the bends so as to avoid the whizzing cars that whipped around them with no warning, all the while bellowing out"Turkey!" and "Who's a good girl?", well, it was a heart-stopping dance with death. The surrounding area seemed so desolate and devoid of humans that it was easy to imagine that the last pedestrian before me may have sported moccasins and a loincloth. But since this is where Zees had been sighted, I had no choice but to keep on looking, and I proceeded down the lengths of both streets for at least a half mile, dodging cars all the while.

It occurred to me at one point that at this very moment, I was supposed to be laying on a blanket on the sands of the Jersey shore with Katie, listening to the waves lapping nearby, breathing in the salty air, and feeling those ultra-violet photons penetrating my epidermis, serving up that first, base layer of sunburn, without which no vacation is complete. I was supposed to be enjoying myself! Not risking my life trespassing in a no-mans-land looking for a runaway Chihuahua! A seductive feeling of self-pity started seeping in my soul.

It lasted about five seconds. And then I thought of ZeeZee. Of how frightened, freaked-out, hungry, and confused she must be. On her own, with no idea where she was, where we were, where she should go, what to do...her whole existence now hinging on how adept she was at avoiding cars and predators, scavenging food, avoiding injury, her survival a minute to minute proposition.

My selfish preoccupations vanished. There could be no enjoyment for me as long as ZeeZee was missing. It brought to mind the Eastern concept of the Enlightened Soul who defers his own Liberation and Immersion in the Absolute until all other suffering souls also realize the same eternal Truth.

Well, maybe not exactly like that. All I knew is that things couldn't be right until we found ZeeZee. We were meant to be together. Everything else was on hold until that reality manifested once again.

And then the third call came in. While I had been serving as the boots on the ground in our search for ZeeZee, Katie had been covering a lot of ground on the Internet. One of the resources she discovered was an expert in animal tracking in the wilderness. This individual, Gina, offered her extensive knowledge of how to recover a lost pet from the wild for a fee from afar. She would be our guide and consultant by phone, available at any hour for as long as it took to get ZeeZee back to us. Katie had made the wise and unilateral decision to hire her, and Gina was calling me to fill me in as to how to proceed.

"Don't worry, Michael," Gina counseled, "if you do exactly as I say, and don't deviate, you will get your dog back."

Now those were the words I had been wanting to hear! There was hope! Conveyed in a voice that sounded calm, confident, and knowledgeable. An energy opposite to the panic and desperation that had marked our efforts so far.

"Okay, here's what you have to do first; you have to call back the two witnesses who said they saw your dog as soon as possible. Did you get their phone numbers?" Katie had. "Good. Call them back and try to get as much information from them as you can; where and when they saw the dog; what the dog looked like…don't use leading questions that would give away any factual clues about ZeeZee; you have to see if these witnesses are legit. You'd be surprised how many people phone in false sightings just to raise hell, or in hopes of getting a reward."

Yes, I would be surprised. Such thoughts had never occurred to me.

Gina continued, " Once you've determined that these are credible witnesses, then you have to go and plaster the areas where they said they saw your dog with as many flyers and posters as you can. Make sure it's a good photo, state when and where she was last sighted, put in all your contact information, and say there's a reward. You guys need more people out there looking and aware of ZeeZee than you have now. And you need to do this ASAP! Get going!"

Like troops waiting the word from their general, we sprang into action. I continued to search in the Darby/ Marple vicinity while Katie called back Meredith and Edith to verify their reports. Meredith was even more clear than in her earlier phone call. Yes, she had seen ZeeZee—a black and white Chihuahua that looked almost silver as she hit maximum velocity—and then Meredith added another, extremely important detail to her sighting that she had neglected to mention earlier. She said that after ZeeZee passed her and the motorist, she fled further down Ellis and then eventually darted off to the right onto Castle Rock Drive before disappearing out of sight.

This was news. In what passed for our own version of triangulation, ZeeZee's whereabouts were now further pinpointed. A new intersection presented itself for exploration. Katie thanked Meredith profusely for this break in the case, and Meredith said she would be happy to go out later leafletting and looking.

Then Katie called Edith, the elderly woman who said she had sighted ZeeZee at Darby and Marple Roads. Only this time, Edith angrily denied that she had said Darby and Marple Roads. This time, she said she had said Darby Creek Road; not Darby Road. This was a world of difference. Darby Creek Road was far from where I had been looking, though much closer to where Meredith had seen ZeeZee. This was an important correction.

Edith wasn't quite finished, though.

"You'll never see your dog again; you know that, right?" Katie was speechless. Before she could think of a reply, Edith let loose with a final nugget. "Lose my number!" And she hung up. Which proves that even wackos can be of assistance in animal rescue. It takes all types.

So, I had been looking on the wrong street. We can only go with what we've been told. Garbage in, garbage out. When new sightings change locales, the search shifts accordingly. It's the nature of the beast. Instead of freaking out over my misplaced efforts thus far, I resolved to make a new, updated lost-dog flyer on my computer, with all of the current sighting locations listed.

The importance of blanketing the area where one's pet has been lost with detailed flyers as soon as possible cannot be overstated. It is the quickest and surest means of getting a response, even if the response might be alarming. I'm reminded of the plight of a friend of mine in Texas, who lost his beloved pit bull and immediately put out hundreds of flyers and searched frantically for days. He was a rewarded a couple days later with a phone call.

"Hey, are you Carter? Listen, I just want you to know, I found your dog. She's okay; you don't have to worry."

Carter was ecstatic. "Oh, man, that's fantastic! Thank you so much! I really, really appreciate it. Where are you? When can we get together?"

"Sorry, man. She really is a great dog! My kids love her. We could use her around here. I'm not giving her back. I just wanted you to know that she was found and is okay and will have a great home. Sorry." Click.

That just might qualify as the most maddening response any lost pet poster has ever received.

Undeterred by that memory, I went home, formatted a flyer, and walked to the nearby office supply store to run off a couple hundred copies. The nice young woman who assisted me was a dog owner herself, and very taken with our predicament. She also had a suggestion.

"You know what hunters do when they lose their dogs in the woods and can't find them, don't you?"

I didn't. The only hunting I had ever done was for antiques.

"If their dogs don't come back when they call them, they leave some of their clothes that have their scent on them in the last place the dogs were, and next day, sure enough, the dog would be sitting there, right on the clothes, waiting for them."

Sounded good to me. I never would have thought of it. Thanking her, I grabbed my copies and headed back home to see what sort of smelly summer wear I could drum up. The hamper was pretty empty, as we had cleaned house before leaving for the shore. The only things in it were my underwear, socks, and shirt from the day before. A beautiful, black and white Japanese design shirt I liked very much, by the way. But apart from what I was wearing, these were the only items available. I had to assume they were chock full of eau de me; a cologne that at least ZeeZee would find irresistible, even if nothing else did. I picked them up and headed out the door. My plan was to drive over to the intersection of Ellis and Castle Rock and distribute flyers. Distributing my clothing was also an option.

On the way over, I decided to check out the new location where Edith had now said she saw ZeeZee; at Marple and Darby Creek Roads. I hoped to see a quiet intersection, with few cars and perhaps lots of dog lovers strolling about.

It was clear that visualization is not my strong suit. Not a soul to be seen, but there were lots of speeding cars. I pulled over and started walking about, yelling "ZeeZee!," and "Who's a good girl?" Got no barks in response. She was either out of earshot or had become suddenly shy. I didn't know how her instincts might direct her, only that she would unquestionably follow them. The opposite, in other words, of what we humans typically do.

I drove onto Castle Rock Rd., where Meredith had last seen ZeeZee. The street was dotted with widely separated houses ensconced in giant swaths of well-manicured lawns. There were no sidewalks. I took that as a bad sign. Sidewalks meant that there were people around who walked on them. No sidewalks = no pedestrians. No pedestrians = no sightings. I tried not to dwell on it.

At the corner of Ellis and Castle Rock, a low-slung ranch house sat on quite a large lot, with a grove of trees standing guard over a drop-off of some sort on the left. I got out of the car and started trespassing, unusually fearless because I saw a building permit on the front door and the curtain-less windows revealed an empty interior.

I walked over to the stand of trees on the left of the house. Just past the first few maples, the ground suddenly dropped down to reveal a sunken, sun-dappled grotto, totally hidden from the street just twenty yards away. It was a natural amphitheater. The ring of earth, stone, and brush funneled downwards to a babbling creek, whose waters spread out into a rippling pool before gurgling out of sight over a bed of stones. It was beautiful.

I shouted out my usual calls to ZeeZee. The usual silence followed. More than usually, it bothered me. That's because, in my opinion, this glen was an ideal place where a lost and frightened dog might go to shelter. There was water, lots of places to hide and sleep amidst the foliage, and it was many decibels distant from Ellis Road and its thundering motorists. If I were a dog, I'd hide there. Then again, if I were a dog, I'd probably be chasing my own tail.

I walked back to the street and proceeded up Castle Rock as it rose to end in a cul-de-sac eighty yards away, yelling out for ZeeZee the whole way. There were maybe four houses lining each side of the street. Saw nobody. The block couldn't have looked more forlorn than if the Rapture had just occurred and the neighbors were among the risen. Why couldn't Zees have been lost in a neighborhood of row homes, or some other place with lots of people? Sightings would be guaranteed. This was a ghost town. Still, I left a flyer in every mailbox before going back to my car.

I noticed my heap of smelly clothes lying on the passenger side floorboards. I gave my shirt a cautious sniff. The faint wisps of scent my clogged nasal passages managed to detect would have to be enough to reach ZeeZee's acute nose.

I took my underwear, shirt, and socks and strolled nonchalantly over to the lip of land overlooking the mini-gorge. Bending down, I took care to place the items in the kind of artful configuration I imagined a dog's nose would appreciate. How I could possibly know that, I have no idea. But my intentions were good. I stood up and gave a farewell holler. "ZeeZee! Come here girl! Come smell Daddy's underwear!" That particular arrangement of words had never before or since exited my mouth. Thankfully.

Back in the car, I called Katie to see how she was doing. She had some news. There was yet another call from someone who reported a sighting of a Chihuahua on the loose in the same general area. Things were heating up! But when Katie asked for more details, it became apparent that this runaway pooch was not our dog. The caller was insistent that it was a light brown, somewhat porky specimen of the breed, and that it didn't bark.

Well, that sealed the deal. It could not possibly have been our trim, very vocal varmint. But it was a strange that another Chihuahua was running loose in the same vicinity. It was more than a coincidence, as we were to discover a few days later.

Katie also gave me Meredith's phone number, and told me that Meredith said she would be happy to distribute leaflets in the general area. I was stunned. Meredith didn't know us and she didn't know ZeeZee, but she was willing to give the only real things anyone of has—time and energy—to help us find her. No strings attached. It was an unanticipated and humbling offer.

I am no stranger to good deeds. My parents set a great example. They lived their faith. My old bedroom on the third floor of their home housed, at different times, two Vietnamese refugee families struggling to get a foothold in this strange new land, America. Later, it hosted a pregnant, unwed mother needing shelter her own family wouldn't provide. Mom and Dad picketed local supermarkets in support of the farm workers, and even cooked and delivered meals for the homeless even while they were starting to have trouble cooking for themselves. Giving to others wasn't an admirable concept they wanted us kids to believe in; it was a reality we were witness to every day. But I had never known people who gave that same level of compassion and effort to creatures in the animal world. Meredith's offer was a revelation.

The last bit of news Katie dropped was that she had arranged for a livery service to drive her back from Ocean Grove tomorrow. This was the right call, allowing me to keep searching while the sightings were still warm.

My ill-conceived decision for us to split up after getting Mitch's news gave Katie yet another chance to say "I told you so!" But she didn't. She was always more quick to forgive than me. Forgiveness, the Queen of Virtues. I realized a lot of things living a yogic existence for ten years. Letting go of a grudge quickly wasn't one of them. I need to grow in that area. Katie doesn't. Somewhere along the line, I had forgotten that. The lack of recrimination freed me up to focus on the next step towards getting Zees back.

Right now, that meant getting together with Meredith, our first volunteer. I called her and we arranged to meet in a couple hours at the cul-de-sac. Meredith turned out to be a compact, middle-aged blonde with an unmistakable air of genuine concern and sympathy. Within minutes of meeting her, I felt both uplifted and re-energized. Help was here.

She started out by apologizing for the fact that she hadn't been able to grab hold of ZeeZee yesterday as she raced past her down Ellis Road. This was madness. Superman would have found it a challenge to collar her. I told Meredith not to feel bad, but she was still upset. She was a dog lover and owner herself, and could easily imagine how she would feel if her own beloved pet went missing. She took a stack of leaflets and said she would distribute them in the area tomorrow before she had to go to work. I gave her our sincere thanks.

Entering our empty house now was like entering a mausoleum. The silence was deafening. For eight years, every time I unlocked the door and stepped inside our modest home, ZeeZee would be there to greet me, and nothing further could happen until noses were joined, fur patted, and ears stroked (hers, not mine)

I called Katie. She was nibbling on some crackers, her lunch at six o'clock. She had some news.

"You know that thing that they have when a child goes missing? I think they call it an Amber Alert?"

Yes, I knew of it. "Well," she continued, "they have the same thing for lost pets. There's a website which can put out a description of a lost cat or dog to all the houses in the vicinity, and also share contact information. Isn't that great?"

It was. I had no idea that such a service existed. Katie had already arranged for a robocall to go out to all the households with a land line phone within a half mile radius of Mitch's house. It went something like this:

"Attention, homeowner! This is a notice that on August 18th, at twelve o'clock noon, a small, black and grey Chihuahua named ZeeZee escaped from her handler's care on Ellis Road in Havertown. She was lost while not wearing her ID tags. If you see her, please approach slowly and with extreme caution; she is very frightened and wary of strangers. Call the following numbers ASAP to report where you saw her. Thank you."

The Pet Alert call was an invaluable discovery; hundreds of more people would soon know about Zees and would be keeping an eye out for her.

"Try and get some sleep tonight, Katie. We're both going to need as much rest and energy as we can get in the next few days." Of this, I was certain.

"Do you think it's going to take many days before we find her?" I could hear the worry in her voice, and the need for reassurance. But I wasn't going to lie.

"I don't know, Katie. We don't have any experience with this kind of thing. I hope we find her tomorrow. It could happen! But if we don't, we'll just keep looking as long as we have to until we do."

"Okay." There was a pause. "I love you, Michael."

For the second time that day, her words touched me deeply. It's funny; Katie was raised by parents who, despite fighting almost nightly, never let a day pass without telling her they loved her. I, who had never witnessed my parents fighting, have no memory of them ever saying those words to me. Go figure. That emotional muteness was obviously rooted in me as well. But this ordeal with ZeeZee was loosening me up. My heart was finding its voice.

"I love you, too, Katie. See you tomorrow."

Tomorrow couldn't come soon enough. Together, we could accomplish more.

I stretched out on the linen-covered desert that was the bed. I used to complain that there wasn't enough room on it. ZeeZee would regularly push me to the very edge of the mattress, so that I teetered above the abyss. Now there was too much room. Its emptiness mirrored the hollowness I felt within me.

I slid over to the precipice, closed my eyes, and imagined feeling ZeeZee's bulk pressed against my back as she often did, almost like a phantom limb. Her cocooning habit comforted her, and me as well. It was the final confirmation that all was right with the world before we both drifted off to sleep. But now it was gone.

I wondered if it would ever return.

CHAPTER SEVEN

For two nights in a row, Katie had had the same nightmare. In it, she was running through a dense, dark forest, crying out ZeeZee's name. She came to a sudden clearing and saw our little runaway trapped inside a wire-mesh cage. Zees was frantically bouncing off the walls, clawing and snapping at the steel wires in a frenzy of fear. Standing over the cage was a uniformed man with a rifle, the animal control officer. He lifted the rifle and pointed it at ZeeZee's head. Katie cried out and pleaded with him to stop, but he cocked the trigger anyway. He stood there for a long while, with the rifle aiming at ZeeZee and Katie screaming at him to put it down.

And then she woke up. It was tempting to just lie there, wallowing in fear and sorrow, but there was too much to do. She had to get herself and her things together in time to meet the driver who was going to take her back home. She showered, threw her things into her bags, and went downstairs to the hotel lobby.

As she sat waiting, Katie noticed a mother and her small daughter enter the hotel. The mother went to the front desk to speak with the clerk, and the little girl wandered over to where Katie was sitting. A fearless and exuberant child, she started talking about her mommy and her daddy. All the while, she was holding something tightly in her arms.

"What have you got there?" Katie asked.

"That's Mimi," the child replied. "My doggie."

"Can I see her?"

"Sure," the little girl said. "Here." And she lifted her stuffed animal for Katie to see.

It was a Chihuahua.

It's tempting here to say that the world is divided into two kinds of people; those who believe in signs and those who don't. I tend to vary, depending on the sign. But Katie is firmly in the believer's camp. Always was, always will be. This was definitely an omen from whichever kindly spirit was assigned the lost pet detail. Katie immediately felt better. There was hope. Although we and our dog were currently separated, we were still united at heart. Miracles do happen. It could only be a matter of time before we were all reunited in the flesh. It had to be so.

The livery driver turned out to be well-dressed man, middle-aged man with a heavy Russian accent. At the start of their trip, he appeared to be the epitome of the cold, macho Slav. By the time he dropped Katie off, after hearing her tale of our lost loved one, he was a sentimental bundle of sympathy and support. Turns out he had a miniature pinscher at home named Ilsa, and by the way he floored his Escalade after letting Katie out, it seemed he couldn't wait to get back to her.

Dog lovers. They're everywhere.

While Katie was being driven home, I was cruising back and forth on the roads where Zees had been spotted, straining to catch sight of anything remotely resembling a speedy, scared, greying Chihuahua. A feeling started welling up within me. It was triggered by thinking of how alone and frightened ZeeZee must be. How had she spent the last couple nights? Had she slept at all? Had she eaten anything? Did she think we had abandoned her? Was she trying to find us? Did something bad find her?

As I brooded, tears started welling up in my eyes. The enormous emotional shock of losing Zees was only now just hitting me. Add in the two days of fruitless searching, and the tears started running over their banks. It was just so unfair! We had tried to do everything we could to make sure she was safe while we went away, and yet failed. Now we were doing everything to try and find her, and failing again. The feeling of helplessness was overwhelming. Why did this have to happen to us? To ZeeZee? Why did she have to suffer? What did she do to deserve this?

I wasn't used to crying. Mainly because I was so out of touch with my emotions most of my life. Feelings were scary. To protect myself, I adopted the stance of the Stoic. And it seemed to work. Usually. But not actually. Unlike water, repressed feelings can instead congregate towards the path of most resistance, with interesting results.

I experienced this at the time of my father's death. My siblings and I kept vigil over him during his last days at my sister's house. His was a peaceful passing, surrounded by love. I shed no tears at his deathbed, nor at the funeral or burial. I seemed to have it all under control.

But then a funny thing happened. I was new to You-Tube, and found myself watching the same video over and over again, blubbering like a baby every time. It was the clip of the singer Susan Boyle's audition on Britain's Got Talent, were she defied the panel's dismissive comments and low expectations and blew the crowd away with her performance. The clip has hundreds of millions of views, half of them mine. I cried each and every time.

It took me a while to realize that watching the video was a vehicle to allow me to access deeper realms of feeling from which I had closed myself. The floodgates opened, and I could express and unburden myself of the grief that lay there. It felt good. This back-alley way of connecting with one's emotions isn't very commendable. It needed to change. And now, it seemed, it was starting to. I didn't need no video. All I needed was to think of ZeeZee, and the tears were there. This was progress.

As I brooded even more, however, my feelings changed from sorrow to anger, as I considered the man responsible for losing her. In a rage, I started pounding my thankfully padded dashboard as hard as I could with my fist, belting out words at the top of my lungs that surely violated local ordinances. It got a little out of hand; I drifted over the yellow dividing lines and towards a honking, on-coming truck. At the last minute, I righted my car.

I was now flooded with feelings of anger, sorrow, and fear, with a shot of adrenalin added as a chaser. Some ground opened up ahead off to the right, and I pulled over and parked. I shut off the engine and closed my eyes. Something was off. Way off.

It was me. I was lost. Not on the roads. Inside myself. I was completely in the grip of my negative emotions. There was no separation between the outrage, the grief, and me. I was totally freaked out, and it felt terrible. The nineteenth century sage Sri Ramakrishna warned that the two greatest distractions keeping men from Self-Realization were women and gold. If he had just included the pet-sitter losing your dog, he would have really covered all the bases, because I was as far away from being in the right place as I could be.

But I hadn't spent ten years meditating in an ashram for nothing. I knew there was another place within me that was calm, even if rage was roiling on the surface. I started practicing a technique for going within. It wasn't easy, and it took a while. And I can't say I dove all that deeply into the sea of serenity I know lies inside of me. But at least I was reminded of the most important thing in my life.

For a while there, I thought it was finding ZeeZee. Which was, indeed, very important. But without the breath coming in and out of my body, keeping me alive, that endeavor and absolutely all others wouldn't exist. It's odd; the most important thing is also the most taken-for-granted thing. Until, of course, it's about to leave us. Then we pay attention.

I paid a lot of attention to this neglected miracle while living in the ashram. One day in particular I was determined not to forget it, actually tying a string around my finger to help me remember. Every time I saw it—sitting on the bus, stocking shelves at my job, eating my lunch—I was reminded of what was most important and put my attention there. The cumulative effect was an evening of exceptional consciousness and a deeper dive in that night's meditation. I blame that old culprit—Maya!—for not being similarly obsessed every other day of my life.

The craziness I was feeling forced me to go inside and focus on that most subtle and vital phenomenon. It helped. The anger subsided and I started to feel more centered. I had a job to do, and it was best done with a clear mind. ZeeZee was still out there, and although it was early in the hunt, there was no time to waste.

The next order of business was to pay a visit to the animal control officer at the local township's headquarters before going home to meet Katie when she got back. Luckily, Officer McClure had not yet set out for the day. A genial, attentive man with a grey handlebar mustache and a warm brogue, the officer listened quietly to my story of how and when ZeeZee got lost, and what we had been doing since then. He interrupted to ask a few questions, and the look of concern and empathy etched on his face as he heard my tale of woe was remarkably reassuring. He seemed quite moved, even though accounts of lost pets must be something he encountered every week in his occupation. In fact, it turned out he was already aware of ZeeZee, thanks to the Lost Doggie website, which I guessed he checked frequently. He was also aware of something else.

"So, you say your dog was seen on Ellis Road, down alongside the golf course?"

"Yes, back on Monday, just after she escaped."

"And also where Marple Road and Darby Creek Road meet?"

"Yes, later on the same day."

Officer McConnell's face darkened just a bit. His next words came out softly. "There's foxes round thereabouts, you know."

I didn't know. And I didn't know why he was talking about them. It may have been his business to be familiar with all the fauna in the region, but what did I care? Unless...unless...

"Oh, no!" As I slowly started to process the terrifying implications of the officer's spare statement, he went on to make it worse.

"Aye. There's hawks, too. Once in a while, a turkey vulture. From what you've told me about ZeeZee's size, a large raptor or predator bird could definitely consider going after it."

Whatever newly-found bravado I had just been feeling a short while ago vanished in a flash, replaced by a numbing sense of dread. Not only was Zees alone and forced to scavenge for food, water and shelter, but she had to do so in a habitat rife with creatures on land and in the sky who were instinct-bound to attack and rend her to pieces. Among the many dismaying scenarios already playing out in my mind, I could now include one whose viciousness made them all pale in comparison. This was a whole new level of fear and worry.

"Are you sure?" I asked dubiously, hoping Officer McClure might be suffering from some mild form of dementia. "Has it ever happened before?"

He closed his eyes and nodded. "It has. I've seen it a few times. Not everybody finds their lost pet, or gets to know what happened to them. But sometimes, I've found evidence that a fox got to them. I usually don't tell the owners. Not knowing is better."

At this point, I wondered why he wasn't just letting me live in my own state of blissful ignorance. I was doing okay before; now I was in agony.

"But what about the golf course, and all the houses in the residential area? You're telling me that foxes roam around there?"

Again, he nodded. "Aye, there's dens in the thick stands of trees both on the course and along the gullies and ravines all along its border with Ellis Road. And don't forget, along the other side, there's the Reserve."

The Reserve! As soon as he said it, my psyche dropped another few dimensions. The Reserve! I *had* forgotten! How was it possible that I hadn't taken it into account? It was so close, spreading out just behind the line of houses that stretched down the long length of

Marple Road. Or maybe, subconsciously, I didn't want to take it into account. Expanding our search zone to include the huge tract of virgin land that is the Reserve was a prospect I was more than happy to ignore. Until now.

What is now known as the Haverford Reserve was once the vast grounds of the Haverford State Mental Hospital, occupying the northern section of Delaware County. Constructed as a state of the art facility in 1964, its complex once included twenty three separate buildings, surrounded by hundreds of acres of woods. It was closed in 1998. Later re-development demolished the original structures to make way for scores of condos and town homes. There are also numerous athletic fields for public use, a community center, a dog park, and many hiking trails; all surrounded by acres and acres of relative wilderness. A fabulous place to walk a dog on a leash. A terrible place to lose one.

And now that the officer had brought it up, I suddenly remembered something else. Yesterday, in one of my phone conversations with Katie, she said she had been looking at the streets and areas surrounding the spot where Zees was spotted to get the lay of the land. And she had said something about a dog park, a Reserve dog park, that she had a strong feeling we should check out. She didn't know why, only that it "lit up." Her intuition was at work; this place held some special meaning for us. What that was, we would find out later. I had said okay, sure, no problem.

But I hadn't really connected the name with the Haverford Reserve. Was it possible that Katie had psychically zeroed in on that locale because ZeeZee was there? Or because something had happened to her there? Could that something have included foxes? I shuddered.

I thanked Officer McClure for sharing this disturbing information; he was just the messenger, after all. His whole point in bringing it up was to urge me and Katie to proceed with haste, don't let up. Poster and leaflet as many nearby residential areas as we could. In the meanwhile, he would stop by and check out the pet-sitter to see if all was as it should be. One needs a kennel license in Pennsylvania if one boards animals. I'd guess the chances Mitch had one were low to none.

As I drove back home, I decided that the news about the foxes was a detail best kept within Team Michael. Katie was already so distraught. No need to burden her with even more dire news. It wouldn't change anything.

I got home in time to greet Katie when she arrived, and to see Boris peel off down the street in his Escalade. Katie and I hugged each other for a long time. This was somewhat of a rarity. Whenever we hugged in front of ZeeZee, she would immediately start growling and barking her head off. It was pretty funny. We were allowed to be her parents, as long as there were no physical signs of affection. But if we hugged, Zees was instantly jealous. She wanted me all to herself. On the other hand, if we started fighting, Zees would instantly stop barking, hunker down, and shoot fearful gazes our way. I always felt bad when I saw the effects our fights had on her, never mind how they also hurt us.

"How you doing?" I asked Katie, even though I already knew the answer. The shadows under her beautiful eyes spoke volumes.

"Hanging in there, I guess. I had a meltdown outside the church in the square, but I'm okay now. I've got to be strong for ZeeZee if I'm going to get through this."

True, that. The pain of losing this vital being in our lives could easily overwhelm Katie. And me! Losing Zees was affecting us both more than we could have imagined. I was now painfully aware that I had been taking her faithful, loving presence for granted.

I was also starting to dimly realize that perhaps I had been taking Katie for granted as well. Routines, ambivalence, and just plain unconsciousness had clouded my perception of her and her place in my life. Witnessing her tremendous love, fortitude, and caring emerge in the face of our crisis was restoring my sight. She was coming back into view.

It's funny; we thought escaping to the ocean would be a good thing. Instead, it ripped our hearts out. Yet the resultant trauma seemed to be shrinking the distance between us. Even our major clash of just a week ago was forgotten and forgiven.

That was when I had floated the possibility that I might take a day or two off from our vacation together to go down and visit with my extended family, who would be vacationing at the same time in the southern part of the state. For years, I had been joining them there for a couple of days, which was often all I could manage. I loved seeing them; they are my family.

How I didn't see that projected visit as a desertion from Katie and our planned time together says a lot about me. I assumed she would be gracious and be just as happy continuing on alone. Katie's deeply felt sense of utter abandonment somehow was a reaction I had failed to consider. Plus, I sprang this possible scenario on her at an unusually vulnerable moment—just before we left, when she was feeling extremely depleted due to lack of sleep caused by her thyroid condition. Katie has Hashimoto's disease, an auto-immune condition which regularly rears its head. My ill-considered proposal and its terrible timing resulted in us having a huge fight.

It was eye-opening to realize how clueless I was. In my mind, I had the best of intentions …after all, I just wanted to see my brother and sisters and their families. But I was again guilty of an old vice—trying to please all of the people all of the time. Can't be done. It seemed, however, that I was capable of disappointing all of the people all of the time. I had it backwards.

But at least I could see that now. And was grateful to have been forgiven. They say offering forgiveness is ultimately a gift to oneself. I'm sure that's true, but it felt even more wonderful to be the one receiving it. My sin was forgiven. It was in the past. Now, nothing mattered besides finding Zees. When you get right down to it, life, and the relationships it makes possible—including those with other species—are all that's really important. Everything else is scenery.

As Katie unpacked her things, I went to a nearby copy center to buy materials for making posters. I was in the check-out aisle when my cell phone rang.

"Hello?"

An excited woman's voice burst out of the speaker. " I have your dog! ZeeZee's right here! ZeeZee's in front of me!"

"*WHAT!*" I dropped the board and tape I was holding and grabbed my phone with both hands. "Who is this? Where are you?"

"It's me, Meredith! I'm here with ZeeZee! She's right in front of me!" I then heard her voice, a bit more faintly, saying "Here, girl; come here ZeeZee. Good girl!"

I was beside myself. I was one degree of separation from ZeeZee!

"Can you grab her? Is she close?"

"She's keeping her distance. I have some treats, but she's not coming close enough to eat them. She's just weaving back and forth."

"Tell her Daddy's here! Daddy's coming! Hold your phone out towards her; maybe she can hear me!" I was yelling this as I was running out the front door of the copy center.

"ZeeZee! It's Daddy! Daddy's here! He's got turkey! Turkey, ZeeZee, Turkey!" I was just barking out anything in hopes that ZeeZee was near enough to Meredith's cell phone to maybe hear me. "Meredith, is she hearing me? Is she coming close at all?

"No, she's starting to go away! She's leaving! Oh, no! ZeeZee! Come here! Come back, girl!"

"Where are you, Meredith?"

"I'm on Terra Alta; it's a street off of Darby Creek Road. I thought I'd put some leaflets in people's mailboxes before I went to work, and then all of a sudden, I saw ZeeZee coming out from behind one of the houses! It's definitely her! But now, she's running away! Oh, no!"

Oh no, indeed! So close, and yet so far! A call of a sighting in real time, although the fact that Zees was apparently escaping was all too believable.

"It's okay, Meredith," I said. "We'll be right over; try and stay there if you can."

"Ok, I will" she said.

On the run back home, I made a quick call to Katie. "ZeeZee's been sighted! I just got off the phone with Meredith; she saw her. Get ready, we've got to go over there right now!"

Katie, predictably, was even more excited and at the same time dismayed as I was. By the time I got home, she was at the door waiting for me, with leash, treats, bottles of water and some sunblock. We dove into our car and sped over to where Meredith was stationed.

I knew where Terra Alta was, but for some reason, had never cruised it. It was only a hundred yards from where the caller Edith had spotted ZeeZee. This was hopeful; it meant ZeeZee was sticking around the area, as opposed to fleeing towards God knows where.

We made it to the cul-de-sac at the top of Terra Alta in record time. Three heavily-shaded houses with driveways ringed its perimeter. There was an SUV parked in front of the furthest house, and out of it came Meredith, holding some flyers. The same, worried look of concern I saw yesterday was on her face again today.

"I'm sorry," she said, as she hugged Katie. "ZeeZee was right here; right up that driveway, not twenty minutes ago! I tried creeping up her, and I had some treats in my hand, but she just kept barking and going back and forth in front of me, until she finally ran away up that driveway and out of sight. I'm sorry I couldn't get her."

I hugged Meredith and patted her shoulder. "No, please, it's okay. Really! We're just so glad you came at all, and got to see her. Now we know that she's right around here, somewhere. We're close! We just gotta find her."

I took a look around. A dark, two-story clapboard house sat behind its driveway to our right. Opposite it, to our left, a ranch-style house sat higher up. In between, and directly in front of us, rose a grey, fortress-like home, surrounded by tall trees, in whose driveway Meredith had seen ZeeZee. Another blacktop driveway ran alongside it and disappeared down a slope towards some further dwelling hidden out of sight.

As we were standing there, two women exited the ranch house carrying cleaning equipment towards a parked car. I called up to them, and asked if they had seen a little black dog running anywhere around here.

They had! Not thirty minutes ago, they had seen a small, dark Chihuahua through the kitchen window,

running around in the back yard of the house and barking up a storm. They went out and tried to coax her over
towards them, but she just barked even louder and ran
away.   That was Zees, all right.

I let loose with a few "Daddy's here!" and "Turkeys!"
to see if I could flush her out. I couldn't. Okay, so maybe
she wandered a bit. Time to spread out.

Meredith, for some reason, felt the need to apologize
for the fact that she needed to get to work. Working for
a living can really get in the way sometimes! But she did
say she would keep looking later. We gave her a big hug
and our deepest thanks.

Luckily, it seemed no one was home in the grey
mansion on whose driveway ZeeZee was spotted…the
garage was empty and there were several newspapers lying out front. Katie and I hot-footed it up the driveway,
across the large back yard, and climbed a small rise to
stand beneath a couple large sycamores where we could
get the lay of the land.

To our left, a ridge of hedges and trees stretched as
far as the eye could see. Behind them, the manicured
grounds of the Merion Golf Club lay hidden. Below
the ridge ran a deep, over-grown ravine. To our right,
a grove of trees shrouded some secluded residences. In
the center, the back yard surprisingly broadened into
a 20 foot wide swath of trimmed green grass which
dipped and rose until merging with another house's
back yard some 150 yards away. A mini-fairway if I've
ever seen one.

Without a doubt, ZeeZee had trespassed on these grounds shortly before we did. She could be near, she could be far, but this was as close to her as we knew how to get. We set up camp, Katie planting herself under the trees and me going to see what lay at the end of the long grassy boulevard. Sure enough, it brought me to the backyard of another house whose owner was also thankfully absent. When I walked to its front, I got a surprise—this house sat on the cul-de-sac that was the end of Castle Rock Road! Down below, at the end of the block, my fermenting clothes were de-gassing my signature pheromones into the atmosphere. The range of territory ZeeZee might now be inhabiting was becoming more and more clear.

Katie and I spent the rest of that hot, sunny day searching from our new base in the grey house's backyard. I thought about how awful it must be for the pets who go missing in the dead of winter, and for their owners. Maybe not so bad for a St. Bernard, but torturous for a short-haired lightweight like our Chihuahua. At least the weather was on our side. You have to look for the silver lining when times get tough. Otherwise, your misfortune, whatever it is—like, for instance, if THE DOGSITTER LOST YOUR DOG AND SHE'S BEEN MISSING FOR DAYS—might have the tendency to get the better of you. Or so I've heard.

That night, we took some pleasure and much-needed sustenance from some stew Katie had made and frozen previously. She is a superb cook; I am her erstwhile sous-chef. We dine pretty high up on the food chain, thanks to her skillful use of organic and locally-sourced foodstuffs. They know us at the farmer's markets, and we're happy to pay a premium for premium wares. Well, maybe not happy, but willing. And it's always worth it.

Katie's senses of smell and taste are incredibly sharp. She might just possess the human equivalent of ZeeZee's extraordinary nose. It's a sensitivity that can often cause distress when she picks up on pockets of smelliness undetected by the rest of humanity. But it is also what contributes greatly to her enjoyment of both eating and preparing food. Maybe it's a sensory corollary to her highly-developed psychic self. All I know is she has an innate gift for using a wide variety of ingredients in unique and delicious ways.

Her dishes were a hit with ZeeZee, too, even though Zees generally could only enjoy them with her nose. We were strict about not giving her human food. Correction: Katie was the strict one. I was weak when faced with ZeeZee's begging, rewarding bad behavior with succulent morsels which delighted her taste buds but be-deviled her colon. The gooey after-effects of my misguided generosity were often difficult to pick up with a plastic bag on our walks.

I'd give anything to be able to give her anything now. She must be starving. A treat for her could be a decomposing field mouse. Or a slow bug. Or trash. We just didn't know.

I fantasized that if Katie cooked her famous brined, herb-encrusted, free-range roast chicken and we opened all the windows in the house, a cooperating breeze might waft its scent all the way over to wherever ZeeZee was and she could follow it home. But not even her super nose could pull off that miracle.

As we were getting ready for bed, Katie turned and asked me that by now familiar question, looking at me with her bewitching, hazel eyes which were both hopeful and fearful.

"Do you think we'll find her?"

I nodded. "I think so. ZeeZee's been seen by numerous people in the same general area. And Meredith said she's willing to help us. It's still early. We just need to give it more time. There's plenty of room for hope."

Now Katie nodded. I could see she felt better. So did I. I was right about where things stood, and we were right to be hopeful we could be re-united with our little Chihuahua girl soon.

As we lay in bed, exhaustion took hold, and yet we were unable to fall asleep. My body ached, and my mind couldn't stop going over all that happened and what needed to happen. There's that phrase—the "monkey" mind—to describe the ceaseless, uncontrollable racing of one's thoughts. Mine were definitely going ape. I suspected Katie's were also; I could tell from her breathing she wasn't asleep. The day's physical exertions were over. Not the mental ones.   I thought about praying. It had been a while. A long while. I prayed a lot as a kid, prayed some in Latin as an altar boy, and might have even issued a couple of prayers in Hindi before settling from time to time on that wordless, primal cry from the heart whose best translation might be "HELP!" That's about all I can usually manage. It's funny; I, who was surrounded by religion and rituals growing up, was unable to pray. Katie, who, though Jewish, was raised in a secular household where food was the religion and the high priest was the Deli Lama, prayed frequently, fervently, and with great faith.

Instead of praying, I found myself thinking of Zees and all the love that she had for us and all the love we had for her. Prayer might be out, but visualization was in. I pictured Katie's and my re-union with an ecstatic ZeeZee over and over again, trying to feel the joy, relief and happiness it would bring. While imagining the sloppy facial that was ZeeZee's gift to me after even a brief separation, I fell asleep.

CHAPTER EIGHT

Searching for a lost pet is a lot of work. No getting around it. There are lots of physical details to attend to …creating and distributing flyers and posters, making phone calls and using social media, contacting relevant organizations, not to mention cruising and walking the neighborhoods where sightings happened. We had been doing all of the above.

But Katie wasn't satisfied with only making efforts in the physical world. There were things in the metaphysical realm which she could do and which she believed could be of help.

Ever since Day One, Katie had been visualizing and "sending out" rays of blue-white light to surround and protect our little runaway Chi baby. She had done the same thing many times previously to help heal friends who were suffering in some way. The colors she envisioned might change according to the circumstances, but her faith in their powers has never wavered. Mine sometimes did.

Another practice Katie was engaging in was to imagine the weight of ZeeZee's body pressed against her, as Zees often did when Katie took a nap. She also tried to feel the weight of ZeeZee's paws walking across her chest, and the scratching Zees would inflict on her arm whenever she was trying to get Katie's attention. These repeated imaginings were an internal effort to lay the groundwork for the successful manifestation of ZeeZee's return. Katie had for many years studied the works of Neville Goddard, who advocated that acting and believing as if a certain desired outcome was already a fait accompli could actually influence future events. If we are co-creators of our reality, as some believe, then Katie was making sure she was doing her part.

And let's not forget smudging! It's safe to say there are a lot of workers who leave their homes in the morning surrounded by wreaths of smoke. But how many of them acquired it by virtue of having a burning wand of dried sage waved about their person? Not many. I was often one of them.

I didn't really mind. It was just another way Katie showed that she cared for me. She has faith, as do many native indigenous peoples, that the smoke from the burning herb has curative and preventive powers. I might have showered, but that didn't mean my aura couldn't still use a cleansing. You can't capture a canine while enveloped in a toxic cloud of negative energy! Everyone knows that!

Upon reflection, I realized smudging wasn't really anything new or strange. After all, I had been raised in a religion where holy water, oils, and incense were all used in blessings and benedictions. The fragrance of burning frankincense waved around the casket during a funeral Mass remains fresh in my mind. Even in the ashram, there was a ritual whereby a cotton candle soaked in ghee was circulated on a tray and we passed our hands over the flame and then over our heads in a symbolic tribute to the Inner Light.

Visitors to our house can't miss a side-table that looks suspiciously like an altar of some sort. That's because it is. Katie has always set aside a place where pictures, statues, candles, herbs, and other items with special meaning are displayed and which serves as a focal point for prayer and visualization. Hundreds of millions of people make weekly pilgrimages to petition the Almighty in front of similar shrines. Katie's just happens to be closer to home and closer to her heart. And she was giving it a workout.

Did I share Katie's faith in these practices? Not really. Having been raised surrounded by the trappings, concepts, and rituals of religion, they don't have the same allure for me that they do for Katie. Plus, I had jettisoned belief systems in favor of my own practical realizations long ago. But I still had faith in Katie's remarkable intuitive sensibilities, and if she wanted to add paranormal practices to our physical ones, I had no objection.

As far as our boots on the ground efforts were concerned, we had little choice but to return to our backyard stakeout spot. Luckily, the owners of the grey house were still elsewhere. As, apparently, was ZeeZee. The only answers to my calls were the distant pings of drivers hitting golf balls.

On one of my ambles along the grassy fairway, I saw an older gentleman standing outside the house at its end. His name was Joe, and, fortunately, he was a nice guy. What else can you call someone who calmly listens to a stranger in his own backyard tell him why he has to basically keep on trespassing, and not only not object, but offer to help?

As I was telling Joe our troubles, I began to hear a far-off commotion of some kind. It seemed to be coming from back towards the grey house. Was that…a dog barking? And…was that…a woman screaming?

At that moment, my cell phone rang.

"MICHAEL! *Michael!!* I just saw ZeeZee! She's back here! Hurry up! Get over here! She's running away!" Katie's voice had risen in range to a breathless ultra soprano that would have made Maria Callas envious. I had heard that vocal register just a couple times before in our lives together. It had not lost its capacity to chill.

"Joe! It's ZeeZee! They just saw her back there! Gotta run!" I flung these words over my shoulder as I started running. Joe waved me on, shouting encouragement. This was no doubt the most excitement his yard had hosted since the great squirrel fight of 2009.

I saw Katie yelling and running towards me as best she could. It wasn't easy for her; her weakened left side made such exertions difficult. Despite that, she was really covering some ground. I kept looking from side to side as I was closing in on Katie, hoping to see ZeeZee and calling out my standard "Daddy! Turkey! ZeeZee!" mantra in between catching my breath. But I didn't see her.

We met in the middle of the trail.

"What happened? Where is she? Where'd she go?" The words rushed out of my mouth, even as I kept swiveling my head in all directions in hopes of seeing ZeeZee. I knew instinctively that every second now was precious. She had to be so close! And yet if she was running away at her full speed since being sighted even just moments ago, she might already be almost out of earshot, no matter the direction.

Katie tried to tell me, in between gulping for air. "I was sitting in the chair…I was texting…then all of a sudden I heard a dog…barking…like crazy! I got up… and I looked over by the trees…and I saw ZeeZee!…just the back of her! She was running into the bushes…over there!" Katie pointed over to the hedges which marked the border of the ravine. "I saw her disappear there! It was just a minute ago or so ago!"

We ran over to the mass of bushes and brambles that edged the ravine and then thickened into a dense mass of foliage and trees which extended out of sight.

"ZeeZee! ZeeZee! Come here girl! Daddy's here!" We yelled these doggie buzzwords incessantly into the silent, shadowed stretch of wilderness in front of us. And strained to catch a yelp in response, or a glimpse of a leg, a tail, or even a bat wing of an ear. But we didn't see or hear anything.

It felt like some sort of a cruel joke, which ZeeZee was in on, but not us. How could she have been within sight and, presumably, earshot, and not come to us? Was she afraid of us now? Or did she not hear us? Either prospect was discouraging. After all of our efforts, for her to run away from us like we were a couple of dog-catchers (which we were), well, that was just heartbreaking.

Eventually, we returned to our outpost by the sycamores. Katie and I looked at each other and didn't say a word. Didn't need to; we knew how each other was feeling. The same as we had felt yesterday, when, for a few moments, there was hope that our fugitive bantam-weight barker would soon be squirming in our arms once again. And then the hope was dashed. It was crushing. If our own pet of seven years, after having been lost in a strange area for four days, chose to run from us rather than come to us…well, then, we were in for a trying time indeed.

This seemed like a good time to consult with Gina, the expert finder of missing mammals. After filling her in on what had been happening, she had two pieces of advice—one common-sensical, the other unsettling in the extreme.

Her first recommendation was that we should set up a feeding station near where Katie had seen ZeeZee hightail it into the underbrush. A bowl of food and one of water. We would stock the food bowl with fragrant offerings ZeeZee never got at home—chicken livers, semi-cooked bacon, maybe some provolone cheese. As an appetizer of sorts, a couple of my well-worn socks and a prized tee shirt could be tossed nearby as well. How could her nose resist?

Gina then instructed us to position ourselves a good distance away from the feeding station, and out of the direct line of sight of ZeeZee should she emerge. The reason why was the dismaying part. She told us that the ZeeZee we were looking for might no longer be the ZeeZee we had lost. A switch may have been flipped. Once removed from familiar surroundings and forced to fend for one's self in the wild over many days, a formerly beloved pet—especially one of a breed as small and anti-social as the Chihuahua—could revert to a survivalist frame of mind which could override her previous domesticity. ZeeZee might have become feral. All bets were off, relationship-wise. Katie and I may now have joined that limitless list of human beings that ZeeZee will either bark at or avoid.

This was devastating news. I had been ZeeZee's everything for many years now. She would whimper and cry whenever I left the house, even just for a few minutes, and would bark and yelp in a frenzy of doggie delight for five minutes whenever I returned. The special bond of unconditional love and loyalty between a dog and its master had seemed firmly in place between me and ZeeZee. It was unthinkable that even the trauma of being lost for several days could alter it. But that is what Gina told me.

And that is why she said we should hide someplace where we could see the feeding station but at the same time be out of ZeeZee's sight. We were not to make eye contact. If she emerged and saw us, we should not look directly at her, but drop to the ground and try to obliquely offer some treats in our outstretched hands and hope she comes close enough for us to grab.

There's that phrase often seen in lost dog posters… "DO NOT CHASE!" Somehow, the rescuer, often a stranger, had to save the animal without chasing it, looking it in the eye, or otherwise appearing intimidating. Good luck with that. Our role in the life of our own beloved pet had been reduced to adopting the pose of disinterested albeit well-provisioned strangers silently beseeching her to accept a treat from a hand bent on capturing her.

Things had just gotten a lot harder.

It was extremely difficult for Katie and me to wrap our heads around this bleak new development. In a way, it was even harder to accept than her going physically missing. Gina was basically telling us that the familiar, loving creature with whom we were bonded was likely already gone. Zees had changed. This was a second, unexpected form of loss, and hurt deeply. And I had been through a lot of losses recently.

On the material level, things were difficult. I was engaged in a legal dispute with an insurance company over what was for me a considerable amount of money. Uncle Sam reviewed a couple years worth of my taxes and decided he wanted a similar amount. To complete the trifecta, I had undergone a heart procedure which left me with yet another debt of the same size. All at a time when my business was going through a downturn.

But flagging finances were nothing compared to the true losses I had suffered of late. Both of my parents had passed away recently within a relatively short period of time. A relative and a good friend both took their own lives. A best friend from my ashram days died from brain cancer, another from an aneurysm. Two close business associates died of strokes. A cousin passed before his time. The lovely woman who was my first partner died during elective surgery. The often-ignored reality that we're all just brief visitors on this planet was hitting home in very personal and painful ways.

Suffering these losses had the effect of making our tight little family unit—Katie, me, and ZeeZee—all the more precious. As my circle of loved ones narrowed, my appreciation for those who remained grew. Katie and I had our problems, no question. But we had each other's backs! And ZeeZee's! No way we were going to give up on her. And if our beloved canine child no longer recognized us, if she had succumbed to some form of feral dementia, as heart-breaking as that was, well, too bad; we knew that she loved us even if she didn't, and we were still going to do everything we could to find her. At this point in time, that meant following Gina's directions.

We laid a blanket behind a hillock on the fairway, where we had a perfect view of the spot where ZeeZee had disappeared into the ravine, as well as a view all the way down to the grey house. I made a run and got the dog treats, as well as some of my vintage unwashed laundry. We laid them out and retreated to our blanket behind the rise, our new home base. For the rest of the searingly hot day and into the early evening, we kept up our surveillance, with Katie continuing her cyber efforts and me canvassing the nearby streets. We felt drained and depressed. Could things get any worse?

You bet they could!

In our call with Gina, she mentioned that we had better hope that the weather didn't turn ugly. In her experience, a passing thunderstorm could often frighten a lost animal so much that it might flee from where it had been living and end up in some entirely new location, often far away. There's a sonic reason why the Fourth of July is the most popular night of the year for dogs to go missing.

Katie and I just looked at each other. This was too much. The pattern of sunny days and scorching temperatures of the past week had been forecast to change this very night into a chance for severe thunderstorms. We had already noticed the building clouds and felt a subtle change in the air as the barometric pressure dropped. By the time we got home, the wind was already causing tree branches to start thrashing about, revealing the silvery undersides of the violently blowing leaves. The atmosphere was sulfurous, the blackening clouds roiling.

This was going to be a doozy, all right.

I couldn't help remembering how ZeeZee reacted to thunderstorms in the past. Even though completely sheltered and with her two favorite humans nearby,

ZeeZee would make a beeline to bury herself beneath the nearest pillow, blanket, or piece of furniture. Heartbreaking canine wailing could then be heard issuing from wherever it was she had hidden herself. Claps of thunder petrify her. Hey, they scare me too, when the strikes land too close to home! But on this night, ZeeZee was somewhere out there in the wild world, alone, starving, and already spooked out of her mind. How she might react to this forthcoming unleashing of the heavens was anybody's guess.

That night, we went to bed exhausted. Too much sun and stress can do that to you. Despite the growing atmospheric disturbances outside, we both fell asleep immediately.

We didn't sleep long. A tremendous lightning strike woke me up. Not the thunder, mind you. The flash. A brief, impossibly brilliant whiteness that filled the room, penetrated my eyelids, and jerked my consciousness straight out of its slumber. Before I could even realize what had happened, the thunder struck, a tremendous, shocking boom that shook the house and set off every car alarm on the block.

Katie let out an involuntary scream and grabbed my shoulders. "Oh my God! Michael! Wake up! There's lightning! Oh my God!"

I was completely awake, all right. A hundred proof shot of adrenalin can do that. "It's okay, Katie. I'm awake. I heard it. I know; I know. It's storming." Understatement of the year.

I looked over at Katie and saw her face change, in a way I've seen it change before. And it's never good. Her large eyes widened and then bore into mine with an alarming intensity. *Uh oh.* I thought. *Here it comes.*

"Michael! We have to go back there! Right now! ZeeZee's out there!"

"I know, I *know*. I know she's out there, Katie. But what can we do? We can't go out there now!" This wasn't just Mr. Logic talking, for a change; Mr. Intuition was right there with him. No way were we going to go out in that.

My words made not a dent. Katie became even more upset. "My baby's out there! She's all alone! She's such a little dog; she's so vulnerable! You know how she hates storms! We've got to go get her!" The pitch in her voice was rising.

I tried again. "Katie, please, I know, I know, it's horrible! But we can't go out now. She'll make it. We'll get her; we'll get her tomorrow. Not now." The notion that we could have any success finding her in the midst of this torrent was beyond laughable. There was a greater likelihood we could be struck by lightning. We are naive enough to buy a few lottery tickets whenever a jackpot grows huge; we must think winning is a possibility. The much greater prospect that lightning could indeed smite us couldn't be discounted.

Katie was incapable of taking that danger or any other into consideration at that moment. She was now in the grip of a fury. And it was directed towards me.

"This is all your fault! I *told* you I didn't want to leave her with that sitter! I *begged* you! But you wouldn't listen to me. And now she's lost! She's out there! And it's…it's…I…I…" Katie struggled to speak as hysterical sobs started to rise up from deep within her, competing for her breath.

I had seen her like this before. I knew what was coming. I reached over, grabbed her shoulders and held her close, just as a tsunami wave of emotion crashed through her being, dissolving the fury, the fear, and the frustrations of the past trying days and leaving her speechless and heaving with sorrow. I held her tightly and she held me back, crying her heart out.

It went on like that for a while. There was nothing to say. Our embrace was all we could manage, all we needed. After a while, the tears stopped, the cries quieted. We stayed there holding one another as the storm outside raged on. The storm inside was over. In between the cracks of thunder, we could hear each other breathing. Breath in, breath out. That was all that was going on. It was simple. And profound. A calmness grew within us. We had gotten down to emotional bedrock. A wondrously still place I wish I didn't need a crisis to visit more often.

I know that a perfect place exists within all of us always, even at the worst of times. I had experienced it in meditation back in my ashram days, and I know that it never leaves me; I leave it. Getting even a little near it brings a feeling of peace and tranquility. And that is where we found ourselves after the storm within subsided.

We lay in the bed, listening as the cracks and booms of the storm slowly faded away. I wondered what tomorrow would bring. The new day could bring a new reality. Our possibly feral, tag-less, scavenging dog could now be far from where she had been sighted, and possibly out of our reach forever. It was not a thought conducive to sleep. However, resting in that calm place, it was a thought I could also accept. We were not in control of ZeeZee's fate, and if it was not to be the one we wanted, we could never have peace unless we accepted it.

I hoped I would be as wise when morning came.

CHAPTER NINE

There once was a Great Soul who lived humbly in a cave outside of a rural village. He had a young man as a student, eager to learn his wisdom. One day, the youth asked the Master "What is Truth? What is real in this life?" The old man replied "I will tell you, but first, please go and fetch me a pail of water from the village."

No problem. But as the boy was hauling up the water from the well, he met a beautiful young girl who was there for the same purpose. Overcome by her beauty, he followed her home and asked her father for her hand in marriage. He may even have asked her!

They were married and she bore him children. He started a business, which prospered. Life as a house-holder was very good indeed. Then, one particularly nasty monsoon season, a flash flood roared through the village, destroying his house, sweeping away his wife and children, and depositing him—where else?—at the entrance of his former Master's cave.

Seeing his old teacher, the man burst into tears. He cried and begged the sage to tell him why this had happened to him, why was life so cruel. The Master replied "I will tell you. But first, where is my pail of water?"

Yep, that's Illusion all right! Circumstances can sweep us far away in an instant to a completely new reality. That's what had happened to me and Katie. As soon as ZeeZee was gone, so were all our usual routines. So long, business! Goodbye, family and friends! Nothing was as it had been. Everything was subsumed to the only thing that mattered anymore—finding ZeeZee.

Her normal routine, by the way, involved starting each day obeying Nature's call in our backyard. Unless, of course, it was raining. Then, she would stand on the threshold for barely two seconds before trotting back in, giving me a look as if to say "are you kidding me?" She would then settle into her favorite spot atop the middle cushion of our leather couch, deepening the sag which was her contribution to our decor.

Katie's usual routine had her out scouting a regular circuit of second-hand stores looking for unique items to re-purpose and re-sell. She has had some big scores. She once got a set of almost new Le Crueset cookware for $25.00 at a flea market. What made it even more satisfying was that she had spent weeks visualizing just such a find. A twofer! Another time, she picked up the life's work of a gifted photographer that had been set out on the curb, neatly stored in old-fashioned, strapped print cases, during our town's annual Set Out Your Trash Week. It was a treasure indeed. She also made and sold her art online, in addition to keeping the household running smoothly.

My normal routine of late involved marshaling forces to help me in my residential and commercial painting business. Occasionally, if I told someone I was a painter, they would mistake me for an artist and ask where they might see my work. I could truthfully tell them that they could see my work on walls all over the city.

In the ashram, my morning routine consisted of rising before dawn and meditating for an hour and then doing the same at night. At the time, I thought a retreat from worldly things was necessary to advance in spiritual ones. I've realized since that the two are not mutually exclusive. You can be lost in a monastery and not lost on Wall Street. One's own connection to the Self isn't dependent on or de-railed by a particular address.

Katie's and my new routine—looking for ZeeZee—was easily the least favorite of our lives, but also the most important...her life hung in the balance. No one would describe ZeeZee as being very hardy. She was a spindly, nervous, picky and pampered princess. She might bark a lot, but there was very little bite behind it. Her best defense might be her speed. But she could only run so far for so long.

It seemed contradictory that instinct would turn ZeeZee feral, when her best chance for survival lay in responding to us. But what did I know of her deeper, bestial wisdom? As a small, domesticated canine long separated not just from her own species but now also from her human caretakers, alone in a frightening new environment, her inner gears had shifted from predator to prey, from fight to flight. Now everything was out to get her, including us. She was existing in a perpetual state of panic. And so, on some level, were we.

Our new routine found us continuing our hidden surveillance on our blanket by the ravine. In the tradition of duck blinds and deer blinds, we made a Chihuahua blind. And discovered that keeping a lookout properly is quite a taxing proposition. A partner helps. You can't just bring a book along or watch a video on your smart phone. You have to keep your eyes trained on the primary target, while at the same time making periodic, sweeping scans in all directions radiating outwards. Can't afford to miss anything. It requires a constant attentiveness that become surprisingly tedious.

At one point, Katie laid down on the blanket and took a nap. I watched her as she slept. The years have been very kind to Katie. The only difference between the woman I met at the bistro decades ago and the one asleep in front of me now was that her hair was longer. Her clothes were different, but just as colorful. Her eyes, though closed, had lost none of their power to bewitch.

She seemed at peace, lying there. She had had precious little of it the past four days. Each one of them had taxed her emotional reserves to their limit. But she hadn't cracked. She had quivered, and she had wept. But she hadn't fallen into the black hole of paralyzing hopelessness that had been her fate when she returned from visiting her aunt. She was keeping it together.

This was something I was learning again and again about her. Despite the emotional volatility she often expressed, when a dire crisis such as the one we were now experiencing showed up, Katie could summon the energy and the resolve to do whatever was necessary to see it through to the end. She might collapse at that point. But she wouldn't before. Not as long as she was needed.

I thought about the tough times we had been having the last few years. In some respects, our relationship had devolved into a clone of that of Ozzie and Harriet's. The only trouble was, we weren't living in the 1950's. Yet we still found ourselves in out-dated and un-wanted gender roles—me the breadwinner, Katie the bread maker.

Trouble came when the bread I was winning wasn't enough. That's when things began to get tough. How tough? Well, there was the bankruptcy. And years of barely scraping by. It's not that either one of us was very materialistic. Some of the happiest years of my life were spent living in the ashram, owning nothing more than a couple sets of clothes. But there were times since when I needed some help. And when things get tight, there's a tendency to fight.

How could it be that we were not fighting now? I'd have thought that the enormous new stress of ZeeZee's disappearance would have us at each other's throats. Enough is enough already! But we weren't. Instead of fighting, we were uniting. What was happening?

Katie stirred and opened her eyes. I smiled at her. We were on new territory. Not because we happened to be camped out on a stranger's property a couple towns away from our home. But because we were becoming friends again. The best kind of friends. They say when things are at their worst, people are at their best. This was turning out to be true for Katie and me. We had lost something precious, but were re-discovering something valuable in return.

Later that day, I received a text message on my phone. It was from a woman named Tammy, who knew of ZeeZee's disappearance from checking the Lost Pet web page of Delaware County. She was active in animal rescue and was offering to help us in our search. She left her phone number and encouraged me to contact her.

"Who was that?" Katie asked.

"Oh, it's a lady who said she'd be willing to help us. I'll text her later."

Katie's eyes widened, her mouth opened, and I saw that now familiar expression of disbelieving shock cross her face. She leapt off the couch and practically tore my cell phone out of my hand and into hers.

" Are you kidding? This is what we need! Someone wants to help! And she's connected! This isn't someone you text later! I'm calling her right now!"

That sounded too much like right. I hung my head a little, as contrite dullards are wont to do, and listened as Katie called and started talking to this woman, Tammy. What I had failed to recognize was just how important this response to Katie's many social media efforts was. She had been relentlessly alerting, updating, posting and pleading on every platform and website she could think of for five days in hopes of finding more people to help us. Now, someone had come forward, someone connected. Just how much she could help we would find out later.

"Hello, Tammy? This is Katie. You texted Michael about helping us find ZeeZee. I'm ZeeZee's mom, and I'm grateful that you called us!" This was the understatement of the year.

"Oh, you're welcome! Please, it's nothing. It's the least I could do. I saw the post about ZeeZee being lost a few days ago. I've been following the sightings. Me and some of my friends. In fact, I gave your number to someone else who also lost a Chihuahua in the same area, figuring you guys might be able to combine forces."

Now Katie was taken aback. "You mean there's another Chihuahua lost around here?'"

"Yeah! Ron! Did he call you? I saw a posting for Macho on one site, and then yours on another. I put two and two together, saw that your dogs were lost in the same area, and figured you guys should combine forces."

Tammy was perceptive. And thorough. She had done a little more digging and had come up with one more fact that would bowl us over. Turns out that the other Chihuahua, Macho, was lost the same day as ZeeZee, and had been in the care of someone we knew. Someone inept. Someone local. And someone we wish we had never met.

Mitch. The world's worst dog sitter. The man who let a dog escape (Whitey!) even as we were entrusting ours to his care. Who lost ZeeZee within hours of losing

Whitey. And Macho within hours of losing ZeeZee. All without their ID tags, even though Zees was wearing hers when we gave her to him.

I'm using the word "lost" here somewhat loosely. Katie thinks both Chihuahuas escaping was no accident. She thinks Mitch deliberately took off their tags and set them loose. Why, we don't know. But suspicions arose when we found out that Mitch changed his story about how Zees was lost. To us, he said she had wriggled out of her halter and taken off. To Gina, our wildlife consultant who called him to get background information on Zees, he said ZeeZee had burrowed a channel through the soft earth beneath his rear fence and slipped out that way.

Really? Which was it? Why two stories? We didn't know. We just knew we didn't trust him. Katie was actually furious with him, but she didn't let that emotion consume her, as it would have in the past. It was an indulgence she couldn't afford. Instead, she channelled her anger into the razor-sharp focus she knew was needed if our search was going to be successful. She also knew we needed help. And sensed that Tammy was the perfect person arriving at the perfect time.

"Tammy, Michael and I have been doing everything we can every day to find ZeeZee, but we're only two people. We're not youngsters. There's so much to be done, but it's just us. We could really, really use some more help." Katie's voice was catching now, as the raw desperation just beneath her steadiness started to leak out. "Do you think it's possible, maybe, that you could help us?" This was begging, pure and simple.

There was silence for a few moments on the other end. Then Tammy spoke up.

"You know, I do volunteering with the SPCA and I foster Chihuahuas and already have several of my own. I don't know…" Her voice trailed off. There were another few moments of silence. "Let me see. Maybe I can let some people know and get them together. I'll get back to you."

At this, Katie started choking up. "Tammy, I…I… would be so grateful, *so* grateful, for anything you can do. Anything!" The tears were flowing now, and Katie started rambling. "Ever since the pet sitter took off her tags and lost her, we've been trying so hard, and… and…"

Tammy interrupted her. "Wait, wait a minute. Did you say the sitter took off her tags?"

"YES! Yes! I'm sure of it. We had them on her. We didn't want them ever taken off!"

Tammy dropped a bomb on us. "You know, the owners of Macho told me the exact same thing. That he took Macho's tags off." There was another pause. Pins dropped. And then: "Okay, I'm gonna help you. Hang tight. I'll be in touch very soon."

Twenty minutes later, a text from her arrived with the contact information of three people who were immediately available and wanted to help. They were up for anything; postering, leafletting, making flyers, scouring neighborhoods, whatever. Other volunteers would come in the future. And just like that, all of a sudden, we were no longer alone. Help had arrived.

We were touched, and so, so grateful. Thankful that these perfect strangers possessed such compassion and generosity that they were willing to give of their time and energy to look for a dog they had never met. For a couple they had never met. Mind-blowing.

Back in my ashram days, we often spoke of keeping "holy company;" which meant spending time with like-hearted souls who shared a common, spiritual goal. The term "holy" was obviously used a bit loosely, as it included yours truly, but it was still good advice. Similarly, when a pet is lost, joining up with a community of animal rescue volunteers is absolutely essential. They will lift your spirits and vastly increase your chances of success.

The poor of India had Mother Theresa. The women of contemporary America had Betty Friedan and Gloria Steinem. Lewis and Clark had Sacajawea. And we, now, had Tammy Feby. If ever there was someone who fit the description of being the perfect person arriving at the perfect time, it was her. For the last ten years, Tammy had been a local force in animal rescue. She would regularly check the postings on the lost pet pages of near-by communities, which is how she became aware of us. She eventually found herself at the head of a group of similarly kind-hearted volunteers. With strength in numbers, the team could always be counted on to do whatever was necessary to help find the latest cat or kitten, pooch or pup, that had unfortunately gone missing.

Regardless of the outcome of their efforts, the presence of the volunteers was always an immense consolation to the pet owners. At least they were not alone.

Katie and I felt that consolation the very next day, as the volunteers started checking in. Sharon was a voluble, petite retired school teacher whose passion for educating children had transformed into a passion for rescuing animals. She had participated in animal rescues for many years with Tammy, and was on board to help in any way she could.

Robin was a devoted dog lover who wasn't going to let the fact that she lived a county away stop her from driving down on her one day off to help us look for ZeeZee. She would also lend us her binoculars for as long as we needed them

Michele and Kevin were the proud parents of SIX Chihuahuas! They, too, lived several towns away, and promised to bring one of their pooches along with them to boot. Who knows? Maybe Zees might respond to one of her own kind, if not to us. Worth a try.

Meredith, who had already gifted us with our first valuable sightings of Zees, was still leafletting in her spare time and keeping her eyes open.

Tammy would be coming, too. She didn't live in another county, for a change. No, she lived in another state! It was a significant drive south to the bordering state of Delaware, but that didn't matter to her. What mattered was that ZeeZee was still lost. All we responsible stewards of the planet could do was to try and save her. Pure and simple.

It seemed fitting that before we met these selfless souls, a visit to the man whose gross negligence, if not actual criminality, was responsible for all our troubles was in order. I wanted to see what, if anything, Mitch had been doing to make amends.

My knock on his door was met with a chorus of yelps and barks. His charges were obviously being kept inside on this rainy morning. Whichever ones hadn't already escaped, that is. Mitch opened the door and welcomed me in with the same enthusiasm one might offer an IRS agent conducting an audit. Judging by the morsels on his tee shirt, Sloppy Joes were the entree of the day.

"Oh, hi Mike. Funny, I was just going to call you." Yeah, right. And I was about to read the entire U.S. tax code.

"What were you going to tell me?"

"Oh, not much. Just, you know, that I haven't seen ZeeZee. She hasn't come back around. I did see some of your posters up, though! They looked pretty good!" He brightened as he offered this assessment.

"Yeah, well, we're trying. Didn't you put up any flyers of your own?"

Mitch rushed to reassure me. "Oh, sure, yeah! Days ago. Me and Sonja. We put some around the neighborhood. Yeah, that was days ago."

I had to take him at his word on this. I hadn't noticed any, but still, they may have.

"Have you guys gone out looking for her?" I was more than curious.

"Sure, back on Monday. And Tuesday! Sure, yeah, we did."

"Not since then?"

Mitch graced me with the look one gives the hopelessly naive. "Mike, I've got a business to run here. You know that. Gotta take care of my dogs! Can't go leaving them to run around all over town, can I? You get that, right?" He was opening the door to show me out as he was saying this.

"Well, I'd appreciate it if you and Sonja could look some more when you get a chance. We need all the help we can get."

Mitch nodded and winked. "You bet! And good luck! You'll find her." The door closed.

As I had suspected, he had nothing new to tell me, which wasn't really a surprise, and was not in the least contrite, which was. He still thought the entire fault lay with ZeeZee. Or with her collar. Or her leash. Or even with us. Anywhere but with him. He was a professional, after all. It had to be someone else's fault.

I didn't confront Mitch about why he had offered two different explanations for how Zees got away. Or why he had removed her tags. I didn't let on that I knew about him losing Macho, the brown Chihuahua, much less ask him why he had taken off that dog's ID tags as well. There would only be lies in response. And although part of me that wanted to unleash the power latent in my solar plexus chakra in the form of a fist directed right at his kisser, I demurred. It's good to keep your enemies close.

I can't say that I left his house feeling deflated; I wasn't all that inflated when I entered it. Mitch had merely lived up to my worst expectation of him. I just couldn't believe someone could be that cavalier about his responsibilities. If I were in his position, I would be mortified. But Mitch wasn't me. Meeting him was a reminder that not everyone's journey in life traverses the same moral and ethical grounds. Sadly, in his case.

Meeting with our incredible group of volunteer rescuers was the perfect anti-dote to Mitch's bad vibes. Katie and I arranged to meet them at the cul-de-sac on Castle Rock Road. Everyone was punctual and prepared. Binoculars, leashes, doggie treats and water bottles abounded. True to their word, Kevin and Michelle brought along Lola, a senior Chihuahua whose lolling sideways tongue suggested a waggish personality.

Tammy turned out to be an attractive brunette with penetrating eyes. Not to be outdone, she exited her car cradling a handsome, chocolate-colored Chihuahua with a prominent bicuspid protruding from his lower jaw who went by the ever-so-pleasant name of Mikey. Unlike ZeeZee, Mikey had the refreshing habit of greeting complete strangers with total silence. I found myself making subtle efforts to appear the least threatening of men; doggie approval was something I still craved. Guess I'm a submissive! Katie cooed as she petted him, proclaiming herself to be in love. It happens.

Tammy listened sympathetically as Katie filled her in on every last detail of what we had been going through. This was not the first time Tammy had heard such a story, but she let us tell it un-interrupted, because it was a first-time story for us. Her calmness made us feel that our plight was neither new nor hopeless, but one which was not uncommon and that had excellent prospects for success.

We formed teams, assigned territories and tasks, and spread out in the nearby streets and neighborhoods. Poles were postered. Storefronts, too. I used my own psychic skills to divine that any closed businesses we encountered would most likely be supportive, and gifted them with a poster as well. Cars were leafletted. Passers-by were button-holed, each one of them sympathetic. I keep forgetting that some folks share Sartre's feeling that hell is other people. For them, heaven is to be in the company of animals. Thank God for misanthropes.

After a few hours, we all re-grouped at the cul-de-sac. Tammy had to leave, but promised to come out again and to continue galvanizing her troops to rescue ZeeZee. Everyone else promised the same. We were blown out. The village it takes to raise a child is just as important in finding a pet. It's a lonely enterprise without it.

The energy boost the volunteers gave us was enough to make Katie want to further replenish our bodies and souls by cooking some good food, something she hadn't done since before we dropped ZeeZee off at the sitters. Too much agita. The fact that she felt to cook again was a hopeful sign.

Eating well and healthfully has always been important to Katie and me. She only got her first cavity at the age of thirty-two, having been denied refined sugar as a child by her health-conscious mother. Katie's kitchen larder growing up featured whole grains, organic produce, wares from the local farmers' markets, and not much that was processed. I, on the other hand, have fond memories of the baloney sandwiches on white bread that often comprised my school lunch, topped off with a Twinkie. Some of us were just lucky that way.

I realized there was a better way to eat later. I was a vegetarian for a decade while in the ashram, and for some time thereafter. The dietary backsliding began when I was on the road for a month at a time in the Southwest. Back then, it was hard to find tofu even in the few Chinese restaurants scattered about in rural Oklahoma and Texas. One day, I said okay to shrimp mixed with my low mein. That was it. Steak tartare loomed just around the bend.

Cooking with Katie is always a relaxing and enjoyable experience. I chop, dice, wash, and follow orders, and she makes the magic happen. The only thing she doesn't grab in the kitchen while she's cooking is a recipe book; everything comes from her head. And heart. That's her secret ingredient. It infused every bite of that night's Thai coconut chicken stir-fry.

The rising moon found us more at peace than we had been for quite some time. The reinforcements helped. Maybe now we could try to let go of some of our worries. Detachment is necessary for a happy life, according to the Buddha. So true. Yet difficult to achieve. We're only human, after all. Katie and I were obviously very attached to ZeeZee. Our peace of mind comes and goes according to what's happening with her. Helpless prisoners of karmic attachment—that's us!

But, you know, in a way…so what? Take away our attachment to people, places and things and you've taken away a lot of our art, culture, and history. We grieve, we celebrate, we mourn, and we laugh. Total detachment might only be possible for the yogi, one who seeks to merge with the Formless Absolute in isolation rather than have to relate to the sometimes obnoxious forms in which the Absolute hides.

I had already lived the life of a renunciate. And loved it! Mostly. Since then, I had been living as material a life as anyone. And loving it! Mostly. There's a pro and con to everything. So I'll take the good with the bad. The joy and love of bonding with ZeeZee, the heartache of losing her, and every suspenseful step along the way to finding her. Detachment would help, but if I fell short in that department, well, I guess I'll just have to let go of that as well.

© Katie Pfeiffer

(Above) **Me and ZeeZee in our favorite refuge...each other's arms.** Photo courtesy of Katie Pfeiffer.

(Opposite page, top) **Katie's feelings for ZeeZee revealed in no uncertain terms in her painting.**

(Opposite page, bottom left) **Zees and her mommy, Katie.** Photo courtesy of Becca Monks.

(Opposite page, bottom right) **ZeeZee practicing for her runway debut.** Photo courtesy of Katie Pfeiffer.

Cute canines and their erstwhile owners. Back row, left to right: Kevin, Katie, Michelle and Stella. Front row, left to right: Tammy, Dann, and Randy. Photo courtesy of Michael Guerin.

(Opposite page, top) **Me, Katie, Dann, and our restless rescuee, Zees.** Photo courtesy of Becca Monks.

(Opposite page, bottom) **Dann re-visits site where he spotted and captured ZeeZee.** Photo courtesy of Katie Pfeiffer.

CHAPTER TEN

"Sunrise, sunset; sunrise, sunset…swiftly flow the days…"

They do, indeed. Life moves at a pretty quick clip even if you're not immersed in a desperate, all-consuming quest to save the life of a loved one. Even one with four legs and a tail. If you are, it moves even quicker. Time is not your friend. It was surely taking a toll on ZeeZee, and on us as well.

Katie and I settled in for the long haul. We had no choice but to keep making the same efforts, over and over again. Our lives resembled a movie. It would be great if the movie was "Lassie Come Home." Unfortunately, it was more like "Groundhog Day," where each day repeated the last. But each day still held the hope that the spell would be broken. And each day brought surprises.

The surprise one day was to discover the existence of an area close to where ZeeZee had been sighted, and a likely candidate for where she might be roaming. The

Darby Creek Trail was a well-maintained path through the woods which ran alongside the meandering Darby Creek. A hiker could easily imagine that they were in the Poconos or the Alleghenies while traversing it, as opposed to a wild stretch of the suburbs. It was a place that could offer ZeeZee water and lots of shelter. I added it to the hodgepodge of streets and backyards I covered on my rounds.

Another surprise was to see our team of volunteers increase by another four souls, one of whom was to change our lives. Ginger was a retired school teacher and Randy an ex-police officer. Both were recruited by the ever-resourceful Tammy. Ginger was up for distributing fliers and scanning the streets, while Randy intended to stay mobile, cruising every main and side road around the golf course and beyond.

I then got a call from Eric, a friend I had made recently thanks to the poker circle I joined many months before. I'm not a great player; bluffing doesn't come naturally to me. I'm the guy who, when quoted a price of ten dollars for an item by a vendor at a flea market, came back with "would you take twelve?" This was the same subversive strategy which helped secure my seventh place ranking amongst the seven regular poker pals.

Eric wanted to help. He boasted that he "was good at finding things." As far as I knew, this talent was reserved for filching aces from the bottom of the deck. But I was more than happy to accept his offer and see if his gift extended to finding lost Chihuahuas. I told him to come over when he could and meet us at the dog park by the Haverford Reserve. Ever since Katie spotted it on her iPad back in Ocean Grove, she felt it held some special significance for us. We had begun spending some time there, giving the numerous pet owners a flyer along with our story. To a person, they all expressed sympathy.

And then we met Dann.

As Katie was once again repeating our tragic tale to a young couple entering the dog park with their whippet one hot afternoon, I noticed a slender young man with a Boston terrier standing just off to the side, listening intently to all that was being said. When the couple left, promising to keep an eye out, the young man and his dog approached.

"Excuse me, I couldn't help hearing what you guys were talking about. Hi. My name is Dann. This is my dog, Franklin." We shook hands. Franklin eyeballed me.

"I'm really sorry your dog got lost. I can't imagine what you're going through. Must be terrible." He bent down and gave Franklin a pat. "I grew up around here. I know the woods like the back of my hand. Used to camp out by the Creek and on the Reserve. I want to help you guys. My schedule's pretty flexible. Let's swap cell numbers. I want you to call me anytime you get a sighting or need any extra help. Consider me onboard."

Wow. The gifts just keep on coming. We thanked Dann profusely, Katie tearing up as she did so.

"Did you guys know there's a hiking trail right around the other side of the dog park? It goes quite a ways up and through a pretty wooded area." Dann was pointing towards the beginning of a path that we could now see bordered the play area and snaked deep into the shadows.

No, we didn't know that. Had never noticed it before.

"Franklin and I will go check it out. Call you if we see anything. Remember, keep me in mind!" And with that, they were off.

It was only later that we would come to understood what a key encounter had just occurred. Sir Edmund Hillary gained international fame and recognition as the first human being to summit Mount Everest. But the world would never have known his name if not for the expert, utterly essential assistance of his veteran Sherpa guide, Tenzing Norgay. The perfect person to aid in that pioneering effort. Thanks to him, history was made.

And now, entering the ranks of Team ZZ, came Dann Furia. He wasn't the first to join, nor the last. But he brought with him not only a life-long acquaintanceship with the lay of the land, but also a work schedule he was willing to adjust to help us, and, most important, a sympathetic heart. The premonitions Katie had had regarding the importance of the Reserve's dog park to our search were coming true.

There was another reason we were fortunate to have Dann's help, a reason we only learned about later. Turns out Dann is a sufferer and a survivor of Bleb disease. I had never heard of it. It is a genetic condition which can lead to the collapse of one's lungs. It happened to Dann. And not just once or twice. He has endured more than twenty lung collapses, eight lung surgeries, fourteen chest tube insertions (a treatment method), twenty-four surgical scars, and almost an entire year confined to a hospital bed! He is not allowed to travel by air, and is not even supposed to run. Severe restrictions on a young man and athlete who used to loved exploring the woods and was on the high-diving team in school.

Making lemonade from this bitter fruit, Dann formed a support group on Instagram for sufferers of Bleb's disease, providing a much-appreciated forum for people to share their stories. He shared his own pain in one of his rap songs. Yes, rap! Dann "Skip Dawg" Furia is also a rapper and musician who has sold many of his compositions to advertisers and broadcasters.

But Dann's advocacy did not end with helping Bleb patients. He also achieved some Internet fame by taking on a giant cable company, exposing the time-wasting hell that was their customer service department in a series of posts on YouTube. It stirred the pot so much that eventually the muckety-mucks in the corporation got involved, with a significant improvement in that area being the result.

A Princeton grad, Dann set up shop as a personal tutor. This is what allowed him the flexibility to reschedule appointments as necessary so as to be on hand to help us. The surprise Katie and I initially felt as perfect strangers came to our aid was now being replaced by the realization that for some dog lovers, dropping everything and coming to the rescue wasn't so much a choice as it was their default response mode. Just meeting and getting to know these folks was increasing my faith in humanity, not to mention making me a better person.

After another few hours of accosting dog owners and canvassing the streets, Katie looked at me pleadingly and asked "Can we go somewhere and eat now?"

I could see the conflict in her eyes and hear the frustration in her voice. Part of her didn't want to leave. ZeeZee might show up in the next five minutes. But it had been a long day, after a long week. We were both pretty burned-out. We were learning we had to pace ourselves. One dog-loving acquaintance, upon hearing of our plight, professed astonishment that we had ever allowed ourselves the luxury of going home at the end of a day of looking and going to sleep. "I would look night and day, twenty-four hours straight, if my dog was lost!" she huffed. Indeed, she might. Hopefully, kind passers-by would find her wherever she collapsed and return her to her home. If you can't take care of yourself, forget about rescuing some other species.

Driving over to a nearby Japanese restaurant, I looked over at Katie and saw something extremely rare. It was the sight of Katie sitting completely still. This almost never happens. Transport by auto is not possible in Katie's world without the radio blasting some R & B, or, preferably, disco, and when it does, her arms and hands begin to undulate and flutter in a graceful improvised dance straight from her heart. I can't help but look over from behind the wheel; the flourishes and mudra-like gestures of her fingers are so elegant and captivating and in such contrast to how she moves about on foot. These movements allow me to see the dancer in her.

But she wasn't doing it now. The radio wasn't on. And the look in her eye and the set of her jaw would not have been out of place on Joan of Arc as she prepared for battle. Which had been Katie's default mode of being for quite a while now.

Entering the restaurant's cool, dark interior after the fiercely hot day in the sun felt like entering the Pearly Gates. We settled into a booth. There was a large aquarium nearby, and Katie watched the idling Oscars and angelfish as intently as I was examining the cocktail menu. If ever a night called for a saketini, this was it. You won't find too many scriptures extolling the virtues of alcohol as an aid to spiritual development. But I figured, if wisdom lay in moderation in all things, why exempt sobriety?

Katie excused herself and went to the restroom. She was gone a long while. When she returned, I could see she had been crying. Didn't take a psychic. Her eyes were wet and red, her lips still quivering. Crying in public, by the way, is not the horror of horrors for Katie that it is for me, as multiple instances through the years have demonstrated. For me, expressing any strong emotion in public is to be avoided at all costs. For Katie, repressing any strong emotion is to be avoided at all costs. Why would anyone do that? Someday, I will find a good answer to that question. In the meanwhile, look out.

Katie said that things had just gotten to her. This enervating search for ZeeZee was exacting the same toll on Katie as had her efforts to help her aunt in the Bronx. She had returned to Philadelphia completely drained, physically, emotionally and mentally. The Temporary Adjustment Disorder she suffered was actually a form of a nervous breakdown, whose effects she felt for several months. Katie chose therapy as opposed to medications as a form of treatment, and she had only just recently re-gained her normal equilibrium.

Looking for ZeeZee—with its daily demands of time and energy in the oppressive heat, its ups and downs, its distress and thus far failure—was posing a similar threat to Katie's well-being. The greatest, unspoken fear was that it would all come to nought. That we would never get ZeeZee back; we'd never find her. It was the underlying possibility which threatened to overwhelm her. Somehow, she needed to find the psychic strength to keep going.

Releasing tears helped. As did the sushi and sake. We reminisced about ZeeZee as we ate, and even managed a few laughs. There was the time she surprised the pizza delivery guy, who had mistakenly opened our front door without us being quite there yet. He was treated to the sight and sound of an obviously demonically-possessed canine, and we were treated to our first upside-down pizza. Wasn't bad, once we scraped the toppings off the lid.

Then there was the time my friend Mark came over for a visit. He was greeted by the usual ten minute barking-palooza every newcomer deserved. Yet amazingly, not very long after that, ZeeZee was contentedly sitting on his lap, which was a rarity. Could the fact that Mark was a good five inches taller than me have counted for something? Could she be that fickle? From her perch, Zees was giving me a look as if to say "yo, shorty; what you lookin' at?" Was I glad to see Mark leave and ZeeZee return to me? That couldn't be. That would be childish.

There were exceptions to ZeeZee's intolerance of others. One was Paco, the elderly male Chihuahua who lived two blocks down. They met on a walk, and Paco amazingly passed the sniff test right away. From then on, he became ZeeZee's doggie BFF. Which was surprising, because he treated her with a bemused indifference. That didn't stop Zees from doting on him, and it was so cute to see her dancing around and being protective of him as well as us on our walks together. If only she could have adopted his perfect behavior.

Of course, if she had, she wouldn't be the ZeeZee we knew and loved, our ever-vigilant Protector from Everything. Whenever I let her out in our small backyard, she would run to each side of fencing and unleash a barrage of high-pitched barks for the benefit of any lollygagging canines in adjoining yards. Being taller than her, I could see that the yards were usually empty. But she didn't care. Why should cowering mutts indoors be deprived of her warnings? Should a bear appear behind our house, it would get the same treatment. ZeeZee had proven, time and again, that she wasn't afraid of anything. Only, perhaps, of us not loving her.

That was the most needless of fears.

Her mood lightened, Katie shared what she was feeling. "You know, I've been thinking about it. I don't know why, but I feel like we really need to go back and put more energy in at the dog park. It keeps lighting up for me. "

"Oh, yeah?" By now, I knew better than to question things that "lit up" for her anymore. But I just had to ask. "Are you sure? ZeeZee hasn't ever been spotted there. Shouldn't we just stick to where she's been seen?"

Katie shook her head and looked at me intently with her beautiful, almond-shaped eyes. The eyes that had me flinching when we first met. How long had it been since I had really looked into them? I was locked onto them now. And flinching.

"Give me a minute." She said this quietly and then closed her eyes.

I knew what she was doing. Well, I knew, and I didn't know. I knew that she was shifting her consciousness from being aware of us sitting in the booth, surrounded by empty sushi platters, to some-place else, some other dimension. How she does that, and how seemingly unknowable information comes to her, is the part I can't comprehend. But I had witnessed her remarkable ability to foretell and perceive hidden realities many, many times.

Case in point…not that long ago, Katie was in a bookstore when a youngish, blonde-haired man sidled up to her. He started a conversation which quickly led to him hitting on her pretty blatantly. Katie noticed he wasn't wearing a ring. But she also noticed something else, which he could not possibly have imagined.

Looking at his face, Katie suddenly saw the shadowy image of a woman's figure, and two smaller images of children. She immediately knew why.

"You should be ashamed of yourself! Why don't you go home to your wife and kids and stop trying to pick up women in book stores?"

The man's eyes widened in shock. The blood drained from his face, and he gasped "How did you know I was married?"

"Because I'm a psychic! I can see right through you. You need to go see a therapist."

Without another word, the man turned and strode out of the store, shooting fearful glances over his shoulder as he exited.

Psychics. Never assume what they may say is what one may want to hear.

Katie opened her eyes. "No. I don't know why, but that dog park just keeps lighting up for me. I feel like it's important; like we really need to go there. Let's go after dinner. We'll still have time."

She was right. The sun had a ways to go before setting. And if returning there lit up for her, then that's where we should go. I was a little lit up myself, after the saketini, but ready to head out once again. Hope springs eternal.

Back at the dog park, there were a surprising number of cars in the parking lot for this late in the day. Surprising to me, at least. But then again, we had never taken ZeeZee to dog parks. Her entrenched antipathy towards her own species would make it problematic. But it seemed that for some lucky dogs, going to the park wasn't limited by the setting of the sun.

We had only been there for a few minutes, handing out flyers, when my cell phone rang.

"Are you the owner of that lost dog?" a male voice asked.

"Yes, I am. Have you seen her?"

"Just saw her five minutes ago! Down at the intersection of Marple Road and Darby Creek Road, right in the middle of the street. Little black dog; a Chihuahua, right? I stopped my car, but then she ran off into the woods."

My heart leapt to my throat. "*WHAT*? No way!" I turned to look down towards the intersection, which was only maybe a hundred yards away, but it was hidden below the rise of the hill. "Oh My God, I can't believe it—we're right near there!" ZeeZee was a stone's throw away!

I put the phone down and yelled at Katie. "Someone just saw ZeeZee five minutes ago, right down the hill!"

I broke into a run, cell phone in hand, with the caller probably wondering what was up as I completely forgot to thank him and end the phone call. Katie let out a little shriek and started running after me as fast as her bulky overalls allowed. There was no point getting into our car; ZeeZee was so close that it would have just been a waste of time. Had to get there fast!

Ever since the thunderstorm, we didn't know if ZeeZee was still in the area or had fled for parts unknown. And now we knew! She *had* stayed! And was just minutes and yards away. A proximity which owed everything to Katie's intuitive hunch.

I ran down the hill and stood panting in the middle of the street, looking up and down in both directions. Saw neither car nor canine. I strained my eyes and looked into the shadows beneath the trees and foliage that lined the road for anything resembling a cute, black blob of a beast. Couldn't see anything.

Despite the absolute failure of all previous vocal efforts to contact ZeeZee, I let out what had become my missing dog mantra at the top of my lungs. "*ZeeZee!* Who's a good girl? Who wants turkey! Daddy's here!" I know we were told that she may no longer respond to us, but what else could I do? How else could I stand out from every other human on earth? I had to try. But there was only silence in reply. I didn't know which was worse... whether she was out of earshot, or whether she wasn't.

Katie came up to me, out of breath. "Did you see her?"

"No, I didn't. I've been calling her, but she hasn't come. I think we need to split up; you take the trail and I'll take the road. And keep calling for her! Even if she's afraid of us now, what else can we do? She's not about to just jump out of the woods and come to us without any invitation. I think we have to risk it."

Katie agreed and took off for the trail by the creek. I proceeded along the gully that bordered the road, stopping at every curve to listen if there was an oncoming car before venturing forward. I called out for ZeeZee the entire time, and could hear Katie doing the same off to my right. Cicadas droned in response.

We travelled in tandem in the deepening gloom for almost half a mile before turning around and retracing our steps. Back at the dog park, we sat in the car for a while, watching the last visitors bundle their pooches into their cars and take off into the night. It was bittersweet watching people enjoying the simple, loving companionship of their animals while our dog was out lost and running wild. We had just been, yet again, so close to her! But now? Who knew?

Katie's eyes glistened in the moonlight. Mine might have too. This was hard. I knew what she was feeling. Another wild ride, going nowhere. It was wearying. We had to catch a break sometime, somehow. But it wasn't going to be tonight.

Later, we couldn't help remembering what bedtime was like with ZeeZee. The first thing she would do was give us both her version of a goodnight kiss by licking our noses. That was cute. Then she would burrow beneath the sheets to end up by Katie's feet. And there she would remain. But only until we had both just managed to fall asleep. Then it was time to bolt back up from under the covers, waking us both, and jump down and trot off to the bathroom for a drink from the water bowl. Returning, Zees would station herself by the bed and whimper and cry until one of us had to get out and help her up. She apparently wasn't one to make a leap in the dark. Back on the bed, there was a repeat of the licking and burrowing, only this time, towards my side. The last thing on her nocturnal to-do list was to usher me over to the far side of the mattress with her paw nails, where it was clear I belonged. Only then could she and we drift off to dreamland.

I used to consider this ritual an exercise in annoyance.

What I wouldn't give for her to annoy me again.

CHAPTER ELEVEN

Katie and I had been repeating the same efforts to find ZeeZee for over a week now with no ZeeZee to show for it. That didn't mean that we should abandon them. It was the same with the metaphysical efforts, as far as Katie was concerned. Just because Zees was still lost didn't mean she should stop making them.

Out of the blue, another opportunity to employ the paranormal in helping locate ZeeZee came from Sharon, our indefatigable first volunteer. It turns out that she was good friends with a woman who was a pet psychic. That's right, a pet psychic. And not just your garden-variety pet psychic, mind you, but one with a national following, and who often appeared on TV. Sharon was generously offering to pay for us to have a session with her. She just wanted to do anything she could to help get ZeeZee back.

Being a psychic herself, this was not an offer Katie found strange. I was skeptical, though. I knew Katie was the real deal, but had no idea if psychic contact with furry creatures was even possible. And if it was, would it reveal anything beyond "gimme food?" Still, the woman had a reputation. No harm in trying. Katie gave her a call.

"Hello, this is Dolores. Can I help you?" She sounded nice. Maybe this might work out.

Katie introduced herself and was explaining about our situation when Dolores cut her off. "Oh, yes, yes, dear! Sharon told me all about you and your poor little lost ZeeZee. Just give me a minute. I'm going to go inside and see if I can connect with her energy. Hold on; I'll be right with you."

A minute or two of silence followed. If Dolores came back barking out a barrage of high-pitched yelps, I'd know she was the real deal. That would be ZeeZee contact, for sure.

"I see ZeeZee." This was shared in a whisper. "She's near water."

Katie perked up at bit. Could Dolores mean the Darby Creek?

There was another pause. "She's by a dock with boats. I see a yellow kayak. She's near a yellow kayak!" Dolores sounded a little more animated.

Katie, however, immediately sagged. There was no way this could be true. Other than the occasional deep spot that might qualify as a swimming hole, the waters of the Darby Creek were so shallow and rock-strewn that even an inner tube would have trouble floating down it. And I doubt a single dock existed anywhere along the Creek's entire twenty-six mile length, much less one supporting a flotilla of boats and kayaks. Either Dolores just got lucky with the water reference, or else Sharon had mentioned the creek to her and she had gone on to embellish it with her own erroneous imaginings. But Dolores wasn't finished.

"ZeeZee is really hungry!" If divining that a dog lost in the woods for more than a week was starving qualifies one as a psychic, then I'm ready to hang out my shingle.

Dolores' voice changed. Now she sounded like she was a little girl, and in a strange, high-pitched squeal, she clued us in on ZeeZee's plight a little further. "ZeeZee, sweetheart…see the mouse? See it? Yes! Go eat that mouse! Go! That's right , darling…eat the little mouse!" Her voice returned to normal and she announced with absolute certainty "ZeeZee just ate a mouse."

Katie was silent. What could she say? This was just too bizarre.

"How long again did you say your dog was lost?" When Katie told her, Dolores became a little abrupt. "Okay, well, I'm not going to charge you for this reading. I have to go now. Good luck!" And she hung up.

If talking with Dolores was supposed to have given Katie hope, it had the opposite effect. She interpreted the quick hang-up to mean Dolores didn't think we were going to get our dog back. Even though Katie already knew the woman's insights were baloney, that negative note didn't help.

Katie's consistent challenge in life is to not let people's ignorant comments get to her. A challenge for anyone diagnosed as an HSP—Highly Sensitive Person. They feel things more deeply and personally than your average person. Being raised by someone who negated her at every turn rather than nurture her didn't help. It can often result in the thinnest of skins, as I have learned the hard way. A joke at Katie's expense, no matter how innocent or oblique, could be very expensive indeed. This hyper-sensitivity was a regular source of friction between us. It annoyed me that she had so little stomach for laughing at herself, that she couldn't take a joke.

Of course, it was me that was the one judging her reactions to be hyper-sensitive. To her, the teasing was blatant and hurtful. The truth lay, as it often does, somewhere in between. It was something we both needed to realize.

Dolores' silent implication that we would never see our dog again hit a nerve. Katie shed a few tears, then pulled herself together. ZeeZee may have been missing for more than a week, but that didn't mean every minute didn't count. Time to get back to the physical efforts!

Which, amazingly, our incredible group of volunteers had been doing day after scorching day. Tammy would drive up from Delaware as often as she could. Michelle and Kevin and whichever lucky Chihuahua from their pack they picked that day would come after work and walk the streets near the sightings. The ever-energetic Sharon was a leafletting machine…ZeeZee's quizzical, attentive gaze greeted hikers on the Darby Trail over and over again, thanks to the numerous flyers featuring her photo which Sharon had taped to boulders, tree trunks, and logs—all ordinance violations, for sure. Ginger came and looked when she could, and Randy, the Un-met Friend, was still regularly patrolling all the nearby streets and neighborhoods in his car.

True to his word, my poker friend Eric showed up one afternoon to help, looking for all the world like General McArthur in his crisp khakis, sunglasses, binoculars and visored cap. The question was: was he good at finding things?

The answer: YES! Within ten minutes upon arriving, while searching by the Darby Creek, Eric ran into a man walking his dog who said he had just seen a little grey dog about fifty feet ahead of them on the trail. The dog stood stock-still staring at them, then gave an ear-piercing bark before turning and fleeing out of sight. The piercing of the ears was the dead giveaway—that was our Zees all right!

Eric called me right away and together we trotted to the end of the trail, across a broad meadow, up a pine-covered hill, and onto yet another parcel of private property, calling out and scanning for Zees the whole way. She either could not or would not answer.

After another couple hours of searching, Eric had to go, wishing us the best of luck. After all, the sooner we found Zees, the sooner I might return to the poker table to be fleeced some more. Ah, the Hidden Agenda!

Later that day, I was surprised to run into our new friend from the dog park, Dann, on the Darby Creek Trail. Although he and his terrier Franklin had come up empty-handed yesterday, he had apparently taken that as a challenge to keep on looking in surrounding areas. He also had a novel suggestion…that we set out some humane animal traps near where Zees had been sighted. Such traps are normally used to capture nuisance varmints like groundhogs, possums, or raccoons, but could just as easily ensnare a small dog or cat.

This was a brilliant suggestion; it meant that the forces engaged in corralling ZeeZee weren't limited by the setting of the sun.

I went with Dann to a place he knew that rented traps. They were of a decent size, and, after about ten minutes in the car, of an indecent smell. I'm not sure if the odor was the accumulated musk of an untold number of agitated trapped animals or the remnants of moldy bait gone bad, but it was a nose-full. The pine-tree air freshener dangling from the rear view mirror wilted noticeably.

After a stop at a local market to get some bacon and beef trimmings, we went back to the trail, baited the traps, and then concealed them behind some tall patches of grass not far from the creek. They might be out of sight, but I doubt they were out of smell. Especially to a starving dog.

Amazingly, Dann offered to come back later that night, after it got dark, to keep a vigil over the traps. I was stunned. This was definitely above and beyond the call of duty for any volunteer. Just knowing someone would be out there tonight—in the woods, in the dark, looking for ZeeZee—was truly comforting. It made me feel that maybe ZeeZee would feel less alone, somehow. It was illogical, but we had entered that realm long ago.

I thanked Dann for what he had done and what he was going to do. He waved me off. I could see he was totally into it. He had made our cause his.

Dann's efforts and enthusiasm continued to surprise us. Somehow, I doubted that squatting motionless for hours in the dark would be something his doctor would recommend. That, after scouting the woods during the day. But Dann insisted he was capable of it, and I had to take him at his word.

Dann was incredible. But he was hiding something, I was to discover much later. Turns out Dann had to lie down for a protracted period of time every single day. He also needed assistance in ordinary maintenance and housekeeping issues. Over-doing things wouldn't be good. If I had known that, I would have waved off his offers of help. We didn't want anyone getting hurt doing this. But ignorance is bliss. Dann would have been the one to wave me off, in any event. For whatever reason, looking for ZeeZee was important to him. He wasn't about to let a little pain put him off.

Nor were we. And to prove it, Katie decided that, after having let him have his space for several days, it was time to drop back in on her least favorite person on the planet, Mitch, and see what he had been up to. My guess was, eating. But as long as he might prove useful, she was willing to put on a game face.

When Mitch answered her knock at the door, the woman I used to know as Katie then metamorphosed into Meryl Streep, and gave a Master Class in how to communicate companionably with one's mortal enemy. For all Mitch knew, Katie was right there with him as far as how this whole unfortunate business went down. It was all ZeeZee's fault. She was a devil, unruly and disobedient. Poor Mitch was just the fall guy; any fool could see he was dealing with a beast that was one part canine and nine parts demon. He wasn't to blame.

Mitch's wife Sonja came out and stood by his side, listening. When she heard the part about there being a team of volunteers helping to look for ZeeZee, her face brightened.

"Oh, that means you don't need my help. Good." And with that, she turned around and went back into the house. Case closed.

Katie told Mitch that ZeeZee might show up at his house, perhaps looking for food. He listened attentively and said that he would, of course, keep an eye out for her. So what if it had been a week since he had called us or done much of anything to help find her? His heart was in the right place!

I almost envied a conscience that empty of self-examination. If I lost someone's dog, "I'm so sorry" would be a mantra nearly impossible to stop. Losing the occasional pet might be an acceptable occupational hazard in dog-sitter circles, but it was a tragedy to us.

Katie left their house dejected. If there's one thing that will always get her down, it's unfairness. Despite there being infinitely greater injustices in this world, this one was personal and also involved an innocent animal, for God's sake! How could Mitch and Sonja be so careless and callous? To think that our happiness and the life of our dog could be held hostage to their unconsciousness was aggravating in the extreme.

I could tell Katie was still upset that evening, as we picked at some tuna fish. She can never hide anything she feels; it's all right there for the world to see. It's one of the things that attracted me to her in the first place. The lack of duplicity. The unfiltered expression of her emotions. The child-like exuberance and delight in small pleasures.

The key to understanding Katie is to realize just how large a chunk of psychological real estate her Inner Child occupies. Pets of any kind entrance her. Candy casts an even stronger spell over her today than when she was a kid, when it was forbidden. She has collected a sizable library of vintage children's books, taking artistic inspiration from their illustrations. You will find many classic cartoons and comedies amidst her DVD collection.

Katie loves to laugh, which is a raucous roar often accompanied by appreciative clapping. Her natural exuberance is often on display when we take a walk. Apropos of nothing, she will suddenly skip ahead several steps with her ungainly stride, then jump in the air and land with outstretched arms and a loud "AHA!" No obvious reason for it. Which is why I love it.

Her emotional naivete can work against her in the wider world, however. She can be crushed when her efforts towards others are not returned or appreciated. She needs to learn the same lesson Krishna was trying to teach Arjuna…that it's extremely difficult to commit a selfless act. The ego always wants a cut of the action. A lesson I and the rest of humanity need to learn as well.

I also have Katie to thank for my X-ray vision. My ability to see through things. Things like social convention and stereotypes. She is nothing if not OOAK, as they say on eBay: One Of A Kind. This is apparent upon first glance. Katie loves fashion, and seeks out vintage clothes and fabrics which she re-purposes in unique and striking ways. Her look, however unusual, is always thought-out and integrated.

It's not for everyone, though. Over the years, I've watched the eyes that watched Katie…their surprise, the raised eyebrows, the smirks. Who did she think she was, this striking, swaying woman, with her crystal-laden necklaces layered over a smock emblazoned with a voodoo motif of her own design and her brightly-painted Converse High Tops? And what was she doing with that guy dressed like a paper bag?

It's all such a game. What's in, what's out, what conforms, what doesn't. In the end, none of it really matters that much. The eternal challenge is to not judge the book by its cover. For an even greater challenge, try not judging the book, either.

I thought about ZeeZee as I lay in the dark that night, just as I had every night since she disappeared. Oftentimes, before sleeping, she would plant herself on my chest, give my face a licking, and then cock her head and look at me with her liquid, solicitous eyes. The look, if translated, said "How you doin', hon? Everything okay? Can I do anything for you?" At least, that's how it seemed to me.

I took her solicitude for granted. I assumed her devotion and aggressive protection of me were just what dogs did, no biggie. Now that she was gone, I could recognize how much she meant to me, how much I loved her. Thinking of her unconditional love for me, and how I had taken that for granted, I felt the tears well up.

Tears are rare for me. I'm not known for the open expression of deeply felt emotions. It has always felt safer to go through life behind a bulwark of detachment and rationality.

I take after my father in that respect. He was a man who showed by everything he did that he loved me and my siblings, but I don't think he ever said to me "I love you." Despite his impeccable diction and formidable command of the English language, those particular words were impossible for him to pronounce. To me, at least. The closest he came was when he said "God bless you."

I didn't hold it against him. His relationship with his own, quite old father was a rather formal and remote one, from what I gathered. I doubt my father ever heard his father tell him that he loved him. The emotional muteness was trans-generational, and continues in me.

But I was learning. My heart, more and more, was demanding to be felt. The tears were proof. But there was more behind them than just missing ZeeZee. Reflecting on all that Katie and I had been through—both before Zees went missing and after—I felt a pang of regret, sorry to have allowed negligence and complacency rob me from recognizing Katie as she is and has always been since the day I met her…an incredible, compassionate, beautiful person. Who loved me. And whom I had been taking for granted for a long time. But at least I could see and feel that now. And resolve that it would never happen again.

The long day of heat and humidity turned into a long night of the same, with far-off low rumbles of thunder, but no rain. Somewhere out there, ZeeZee was probably cowering. It was my last thought as the physical and emotional stresses of the day did me in.

Behind an overgrown blind of brambles and hedges, Dann crouched in the deepening darkness and strained to see the outlines of the camouflaged trap sitting fifteen yards away. Little moonlight escaped the cloud cover, forcing him to also use his sense of hearing to try and detect any activity in that direction. Although the sounds of distant cars subsided at nighttime, an orchestra of croaking, whirring and buzzing noises rose up to take their place. It wasn't like Dann thought it would be. He thought he would be alone. His imagination neglected to include the swarms of mosquitos and gnats who also called the Creek home, and who were apparently volunteering along with him.

An hour into his vigil, he heard voices. Against all expectations, it seemed a couple were strolling up the trail towards him. This was scary. What if they saw him hiding? Would they freak out? Cause a scene? Call the cops?

Dann closed his eyes. Maybe it would help. He could hear their voices draw near, then gradually retreat. He was safe. With the threat of discovery gone, he could concentrate again on the trap. Once, he thought he saw a small, waddling shape come near it, only to meld quietly into the blackness. Other than that, the area seemed to be completely deserted. Maybe ZeeZee and the Darby Creek's other denizens had already called it a night.

After another hour, Dann did too. He got up wincing. The permanent nerve damage resulting from his battle with Bleb disease flared up with a vengeance. He limped his way back to where he had parked his car. Tomorrow would be another day. Helping others. Especially us. And ZeeZee.

There were a thousand other things Dann could have been doing that evening. All of them more physically enjoyable than what he had chosen to do. But none of them would have filled that space in his heart that only a selfless act could satisfy.

Okay, maybe committing a selfless act was as hard for Dann as it is for the rest of us. Who knew what he was getting out of it? But his actions sure came close in my book. And they were in service not just to us, but to an animal, no less! A dog! How does one measure the merit of such a man? Or woman?

Inadequately, I'm sure. But no matter. The volunteers weren't looking for approbation. They were looking for ZeeZee. Katie and I knew they were special. And that would have to be enough.

CHAPTER TWELVE

Somewhere, deep in the woods of Havertown, our formerly devoted, formerly nine pounds, and forever cherished Chihuahua sought cover. Nothing—no sight, no smell, no sound—was familiar or offered any comfort. She was a warrior cut off from her clan and cast into the land of her enemies. Her foes weren't limited to hawks and foxes; the lumbering, two-legged lummoxes she normally barked at now included Katie and me as well. So what if we had been her parents for seven long years? Dumping her in the house of that stranger and leaving, perhaps never to return, put an end to that fairy tale. Now we were just another two humans to be avoided—every man a danger, every woman a threat.

Looking for any sort of information that might help us, I did a little research and found that some 44% of U.S. households, 60 million in number, have a dog. Thirty-five percent have cats. Fifteen percent of dog and cat owners experience the pain of losing their pet. So millions of people have gone through the same thing we were going through!

For lost dogs, the common ways in which they were reunited with their owners were by searching the neighborhood and them returning on their own. Cats' self-return was their most common means of re-uniting. You get the feeling that sometimes cats just might feel that they need a break, a little "me" time," and off they go on sabbatical, returning at their leisure.

There was one more statistic, however, which gave me a chill. Of the six million companion animals which enter U.S. shelters each year—3.3 million dogs, 3.2 million cats—1.5 million are euthanized. Six hundred and seventy thousand dogs killed each year. If ZeeZee somehow entered that system, that could be her fate. It was one which Katie tried to stave off by her daily contacts with the local shelters, but it would only take a glitch or a slip in the system for that fate to befall ZeeZee should someone bring her there. She could perish if never found, and she could perish even if found. Those were the stakes.

It was why we were doing everything we could to find her. Even if it was something we really didn't want to do. Like the time late one day when two calls came in to report a sighting, only they were both at least a mile from all our other sightings. Should we believe them? If they were accurate, it meant ZeeZee had traveled across busy intersections into distant neighborhoods. It also meant we had to abandon our now-familiar search areas to go somewhere new and start all over again.

I really didn't feel like doing that. Hey, it just didn't "light up" for me! But Katie helped me realize it was something we had to do. This was a role she had played many times in my life…helping me to see and do the right thing. I would balk, I would resist, I would complain, but, in the end, I could see that, most of the time, what she was encouraging me to do needed doing. Her support was that of a true friend. And I appreciated it. A lot.

In this case, she was right to insist that we couldn't afford the luxury of ignoring these latest, far afield sightings. All of our progress so far was due to folks who cared enough to call in when they thought they saw our dog. Who were we to dismiss them now? If ZeeZee had moved, so must we.

But would our newly-formed team of dedicated volunteers be willing to go out once again on patrol, in a new area, at night, with little or no notice? Could we count on them?

Had I learned nothing about these folks? To a person, they responded as if we had just invited them to a free dinner and drinks at the best restaurant in town. Michelle and Kevin came with one of their Chi-babies, just in case he/she could prove useful. Ginger and Sharon came with leashes and treats. Dann—he of the damaged lungs and heroic heart—arrived with vim and vigor. Randy, whom we had yet to meet, couldn't make it, but he gave a large stack of updated flyers he had made on his own to Sharon for distribution.

We all met at the commercial district where Zees had supposedly been spotted and spread out from there. We walked, talked, looked, and leafletted on new streets, alleyways, and neighborhoods until it got too dark. Katie and I thanked everyone from the bottom of our hearts for their efforts, and each one of them said they were happy to do it and would do so again.

Who *were* these people? Their passion and concern for the welfare of an animal in need continued to astonish me. Animal rescuers comprise a secret society—blending in with the general populace, just your average guy or gal next door, until a dog or cat goes missing, and then suddenly KAPOW! A friend you never knew and yet desperately needed comes out of the woodwork to help.

It reminds me of the story of Paramahansa Yogananda's arrival in America from India in 1920 to attend a religious conference. He was an early advocate and teacher of meditation techniques. His ship docked and all the passengers disembarked. Eventually, he was left standing alone at the pier with his suitcase, conspicuous thanks to his robes and turban. A nearby man who had watched the ship unload and Yogananda remain came up to him after some time had passed and asked if he was okay.

"I am waiting for my friend." Yogananda replied.

"Who's your friend?"

"You are my friend."

This response was so unexpected and touching that the man was compelled to help the swami get to where he would be staying. Animal rescue people are like that man on the wharf... strangers until a pet is lost, and indispensable thereafter.

And it's a good thing, too, because we needed their help the very next day. Shortly after Katie and I arrived at the dog park, my cell phone rang. Even before it got to my ear, I heard a woman's frantic cry. "I saw your dog! I saw your dog!" The voice was high-pitched, excited, and a little hard to understand. I talked with her for a minute and got her to calm down and tell me her story.

Her name was Cindy. She was driving back home from a run to a convenience store when something darted on the road in front of her. It moved so quickly she barely had time to swerve and brake. At first, she thought it was a fox. But as it emerged again and trotted back onto the tarmac, she saw that it was a black and grey Chihuahua and realized it must be the same missing Chihuahua whose muzzle she had been seeing on flyers on her street for the past week and a half. It was ZeeZee! Had to be!

Realizing that time was of the essence, Cindy sped towards the neatest telephone pole sporting ZeeZee's mug to get our phone number. By the time she reached me, the sighting was ten minutes old. And I was just three minutes away.

The kicker came when she told me where she had seen ZeeZee. This had all happened on Ellis Road. ELLIS ROAD! The very same road Meredith saw our cheeky Chihuahua streaking down the middle of ten days ago! The same road that connects with Castle Rock, with the secret grotto, where she had also been sighted.

I was elated—this was terrific news! Yesterday, we were worried that Zees was headed towards some distant, unknown territory, and had started to follow her. Today, thanks to Cindy, we knew Zees was still smack dab in the heart of all of our previous sightings. This was key.

I zoomed over to Ellis Road, parked, and started running up the street, bellowing out ZeeZee's name even if she didn't know it anymore. Within minutes, a speeding dark sedan came barreling down the road towards me before screeching to a stop in the middle of the road. The tinted window slid down and a dark-haired man I had never seen before said "Yo, are you Michael?"

It turned out to be Randy, the mysterious Un-met Friend and road warrior, who had already been out scouring the streets for ZeeZee for several days now, even though he had never before met her, Katie, or me. Randy had gotten a call about Cindy's sighting from Katie and sped right over.

"I'm gonna check out all the roads around here; see if I can find her" he said.

Sounded great to me. ZeeZee had been seen more often on roads than anywhere else, so why not keep looking there? Made sense.

"Okay, man, and hey, thanks a lot!" Randy gave me a thumbs up and roared off.

The Lone Ranger had nothing on Randy, in my book.

Cindy said that she saw ZeeZee dart off the road and disappear onto the grounds of a large white house with plantation-style porch columns set behind an expansive front lawn. I saw such a house on my right, and gingerly began exploring its grounds. Just because I had become an expert serial trespasser of late didn't mean it hadn't stopped giving me the willies. In the course of my exploration, I discovered a) acres of woods behind the house, b) a spooky, deserted compound of deteriorating structures built into the side of a hill, which would be perfect shelter for a castaway canine. Or an escaped convict. c) an abandoned car, d) rusted machinery, and e) no ZeeZee.

As I walked back to my van, I saw a figure walking up across the street, dodging the cars just as I had. It was Dann. Like Randy, he had just been contacted by Katie and had immediately dropped everything to come over and search while the sighting was hot. I filled him in, and he decided to go back across the street and search the woods behind the deserted compound.

I've always thought of myself as being a compassionate person. Meeting Dann, and the other volunteers, showed me that as far as extending myself to alleviate the suffering of my fellow creatures was concerned, I had a long way to go. I learned much later that Dann had planted himself in an inconspicuous spot amongst the trees in the woods and surveilled the area for another couple hours. You just can't keep a good Dann down.

Late that day, a chance encounter touched Katie's heart deeply. She was in front of Joe's house when she saw a car slowly circling the cul-de-sac. The driver was a middle-aged woman with grey hair, kind eyes, and a cigarette dangling from her mouth. Katie had a sudden hunch, waved for the woman to stop, and came up to her window.

"Excuse me, but do you know about the Chihuahua that's been lost around here?"

The woman gave a smile and a nod. "Sure do, sure do. That's what I'm doing right now… looking for her. I know all about it. ZeeZee, right?"

"You *are*? Oh my God, that's incredible! Thank you so much! I'm ZeeZee's mom!" Katie was overcome to discover that a total stranger was out there looking for our dog, completely unbeknownst to us. How did that happen?

Turns out, it happened because this woman was friends with both Randy and Ginger, and had joined them on many search and rescue missions in the past. She had been following the updates about ZeeZee's sightings on the Lost Pet website of the county, which is why she came up by Joe's house. And she had a message for Katie.

"Listen, hon, I want to tell you something. I want you to know that I've been looking for your dog all this time, ever since I first heard that it was missing. What you probably don't know is that I'm not the only one. There are other folks out there looking. You're probably not going to hear from them. They won't come up to you or call you on the phone, or post something on your Facebook page or whatever. But I know they're out there, quietly looking for your dog. Everyone knows about it and we all care." She paused to let the next part sink in. "You think you're all alone in this, but you're not. You're not. That's the truth. You need to know that."

Thankfully, the thousand or so objects in Katie's fanny belt included a packet of Kleenex. She started to cry as she thanked the woman both for her efforts and her inspiring message. The woman had managed to zero in on exactly what Katie had been experiencing for a long time. It was a feeling of isolation. Pure and simple loneliness. Despite there being a Team ZeeZee, most of the time, Katie was by herself. And it was getting to her.

That's what made the woman's comment so touching. It was a powerful refutation of any notion that Katie was all alone in this fight. Far from it; there were even more people out there looking than we ever imagined. It was an instantly uplifting statement.

As they chatted a bit more, Katie became even more inspired. Turns out, the woman had recently lost her job. The apparent silver lining was that it gave her more time to care for her elderly mother, volunteer at the animal shelter, care for her own dogs, and, incidentally, look for ours!

Animal lovers. May I say it again? Their hearts are HUGE!

Before saying goodbye, Katie asked the woman her name. She smiled and said "Faith."

Now it was Katie's turn to smile. She didn't wonder if this was a sign. She knew it was. And just the sort of good omen needed to re-charge her psychic batteries and give her the strength to return to the hunt. Faith told her to hang in there and took off back down the road.

Another omen arrived an hour later. An apologetic-sounding man called to report that a few times in the past several days, he had seen a little dog matching ZeeZee's description in the evening on the road at the intersection Lawrence and Darby Creek Roads. He had seen a flyer somewhere, and it came immediately to mind when he caught sight of a small, dark creature scampering along the street as he was driving home from work. The first time he saw her, the connection was made in a flash and, unfortunately, lost in a flash as soon as he arrived home. Same thing happened the next night. It took the third sighting for him to track down a flyer, get our phone number, and call in. He sounded contrite; he knew he should have called earlier. But better late than never. We were grateful.

Katie and I reflected on this new information. The fact that the sightings repeatedly took place on the same busy street at night was both dismaying and promising. Dismaying because survival for ZeeZee was tough enough without her dallying in traffic at night. Promising because if she had shown up there three nights in a row, chances were she would again. I knew I had to go there, just in case. I called Dann to see if he was up for joining me. Well, what else might a hurting, busy, relative stranger want to do with his evening other than traipse around on a dark roadway looking for my dog?

Of course he would come! We arranged to meet at eight o'clock that night by the traps.

Before I left that evening, Katie got a call from Veronica, one of her soul sisters and a reliable shoulder on which to cry. Katie shared everything that we had been doing and everything that she had been feeling.

Veronica took it all in, and afterwards, in a voice without a shred of doubt, she told Katie that we would find our dog. How could she be so certain? Because she was praying to Saint Anthony, and he had never failed her.

"I have prayed to St. Anthony three times in my life, and each time I've asked, he has helped me. Don't worry. I know you'll find ZeeZee. I just know it." Veronica was a chemist, and for one as familiar with scientific method as she, such faith was surprising.

Now, I had prayed to Saint Anthony (patron saint of lost objects) in the past as well, although the last time might have been when I was in the seventh grade. Alexandra's words didn't offer me much comfort. But they did to Katie. I'm certain that Katie, being Jewish, had never prayed to St. Anthony before, but something told me he was about to join Buddha, Ganesh, Lakshmi and Lady Eleanor (Katie's spirit guide) in her pantheon of gods and goddesses who might be of some influence in this matter. For someone who puts her faith in fortunes found in Chinese cookies, no matter how ungrammatical, praying to a new guy in the sky would be no biggie. I once got a fortune with the hopeful message "You will presently be dealing from a full deck." Still waiting, but that doesn't mean they can't offer inspiration.

An extra dose of smudging preceded my leaving the house that evening. It could be a little dicey out there. I grabbed a flashlight and headed for the car. By the time I met Dann by the traps, the late August twilight was rapidly darkening. We decided to station ourselves at opposite ends of Darby Creek Road, with me taking the intersection near Lawrence Road, where the caller said he had seen Zees.

I parked and remained in my car for several minutes. There were no streetlights, and whatever faint moonlight escaped the clouds was blocked by the thick canopy of tree tops. The only flickering of light came from malingering lightening bugs. It was more than a little foreboding.

I sat and called for ZeeZee. But not out loud. I was using my telepathic voice. Why not? Eleven days of using my vocal cords to try and reach her had brought zero response. Maybe if I got really centered and broadcast a psychic greeting, ZeeZee's supernatural senses would pick up on it. Worth a try!

Didn't work. I got out and started tentatively working my way down the road, leaning in towards the earth embankments and dense bushes as much as possible. Every time a car whizzed by, I had to quickly flatten myself against the berm. Every step on this black road this black night felt scary and dangerous. I was squinting all the while, hoping to see Zees, and calling her name, but neither saw nor heard anything in response.

I managed to get all the way down to Dann's territory, turned around, and headed back. At one point, I left the road to hike over and stand by the waters of Darby Creek. It was beautiful there. A bit of moonlight glimmered in the waters, and the air smelled of marsh and moss. The leaves rustled, the stream gurgled, gnats buzzed, cicadas droned, and frogs croaked. This was a nightly symphony rarely heard, by me at least. There was a stillness at its heart, beckoning me to go within. I closed my eyes and gave it a try.

I opened them a few minutes later. Nothing had changed. On the outside, that is. Mosquitos were still having their way with me. But my mind had quieted. Think that's nothing? Give it a try. It will become immediately apparent that our thoughts are in control of us, and not the other way around. They are like horses, which, after running wild in the fields all day, are very hard to get back in the corral. If you're able to slow them down from a gallop to a canter, well, Grasshopper, that's huge! They don't usually stop for nobody.

Taking a moment to pause and go within is my way of hitting the re-set button. Things get crazy in life—stuff happens, often unfairly, and then *whoosh!*...there goes one's peace of mind. We get taken for a ride. But why stay in that unhappy mind-set a minute longer than necessary? It feels so bad. I'm grateful for the fact that I know a way out. A way in, actually. And it has never failed me.

Standing there in the dark by the stream, with my mind at rest, I got the very elemental feeling that I, too, am just a creature, just another denizen of the dark. I was a part of all that was around me. The only creature wearing clothes, perhaps, but that didn't make me better or worse than all the others. We were all just being. I was grateful to be reminded of that simple reality.

Newly restored, I returned to my car. A voice inside was shouting to go back out there and walk the circuit again. I recognized that voice—it was Mr. Logic. Happily, for once, he was drowned out by a louder voice, Mr. Intuition. Going out there again just didn't feel right. My safety counted for something. I kept an eye on the road from the safety of my car for another hour and then returned home.

As Katie and I talked about how things were going and how we were feeling, we realized that something had changed. After enduring so much stress for so long, our emotional reserves were almost depleted. We were running on fumes. There was one thing we were both holding out for. It wasn't as ambitious as wanting Zees captured. But it was where we were at.

We wanted closure.

This endeavor of ours had to come to an end at some point. We could not put off the real world forever. Tomorrow was Friday, the start of the end-of-summer Labor Day weekend. I could not stave off the responsibilities of being a boss and a business owner after that. I would have to go back to rendering unto Caesar and stop rendering unto ZeeZee. I had already lost a number of jobs and couldn't afford to lose any more. My guys were counting on me.

Katie, too, had to return to her projects and work on the Internet. More importantly, she had to take care of herself. The intense focus and energy she had been expending for so long had come close to completely sapping her emotionally. Katie was teetering on the edge of that black hole of despair from which she had only recently emerged. She couldn't go on much longer.

Could ZeeZee? Or was she, too, virtually depleted? She had to be quite weak by now. When had she last eaten, and what was it? I once fasted for five days and felt better afterwards than I did before, so I knew going without solid sustenance was not immediately debilitating. But I'm not a dog. And Zees had been going without for much longer. She had to be less able to fend for herself, more prone to injury, an easier target for predators, and, conceivably, less likely to be sighted. Less likely to be rescued?

Ideally, closure would mean we would be reunited with ZeeZee. But it could come in other ways. It could come with discovering that she didn't make it. Or we could find her in such a condition that putting her down would be the only merciful option. But the worst outcome would be if we never found her and never found out what had happened to her. That would be a scar that would never heal, especially for Katie. Hurtful events from long ago maintain their power to wound her even to this day.

Late that night, I went upstairs and quietly approached the bed, in case Katie was sleeping. As I drew near, I could see she was awake, and staring up at the ceiling. Her face seemed puffy and red, and when she turned to look at me, her expression was uncharacteristically devoid of emotion.

"I don't think I can go on, Michael." She said this calmly. The lack of feeling in her tone was eerie. Nothing usually escaped her lips that wasn't imbued with an excess of spirit. This wasn't like her. "My throat is sore and I can hardly move."

I stood there, looking at her. A woman I had seen for twenty-five years, or maybe not at all. Someone who had just given her all, every ounce of energy she could muster, no matter the voices inside telling her to give up, to find and rescue a difficult dog who could be counted on to immediately take her for granted the moment she might succeed. The entire enterprise suddenly seemed devoid of sense. This was nuts. Insanity has been defined as repeating the same actions over and over and expecting a different result. The perfect definition of what we had been doing the last eleven days. We shouldn't be endlessly driving ourselves crazy like this, should we? Especially in an effort that seemed increasingly hopeless. That's not what reasonable people do, is it?

And suddenly, I got it. Us. Her. The whole picture. It wasn't Katie's reasonableness that drew me to her in the first place. Far from it. It was the universe of emotion she embodied. Yes, sometimes it could overwhelm me. But that is more a reflection on my reserve than her expression. I was the one overly concerned with appearances, how our relationship might look to others. It wasn't always nice and neat, or "normal." Whatever that is. We were in the dark about it ourselves half the time. Which left too large an opening for ambivalence and carelessness to enter. And enter they did.

But our trials these last many days enabled me to see once again a side of Katie which had always touched me deeply. It was her unstinting, total giving of herself to that which she loved. And I realized that ZeeZee wasn't the only object of such heartfelt devotion. I was too. Always had been. I always knew that, but hadn't always acknowledged it. And I was also realizing that the feeling had always been mutual. I loved her too. Joining together to save our lost dog had ended up bringing us back together and saving our lost love. The most important thing had already been found. Now we just needed to find ZeeZee.

Brings to mind Michael's Maxim Number Three: Forget Maxims! Follow your heart.

I lay beside Katie and we held each other tight. I visualized transferring my energy to hers. I am not the visualization whiz that she is, but I tried. We would both need all the energy we could find in the morning. Time was running out. The pressure was on. And ZeeZee's life lay in the balance. We could not let her down.

Contemplating that disturbing possibility, we succumbed to a restless, fitful slumber.

CHAPTER THIRTEEN

It's said that it is darkest before the dawn. Katie and I were definitely scraping the bottom of our reserves. Just in time, our luck was about to turn, and we would be forever grateful.

Friday. Payday. Although I hadn't been working, my guys had been. I suited up in my painter's whites before heading out to meet with my foreman, Greg. Experience had long ago taught me that I dare not venture into the field wearing clothes I cared anything about. That way lay ruin.

When Katie came down, she looked how she felt, which was burnt out. These past eleven days had been harder on her than on me. The physical ordeal was one thing; we were usually moving around on our feet all day long in relentless heat. But the toll exacted by stress and worry was much greater. Katie had lost ten pounds, her nights were restless, and she was fighting a sore throat. She really didn't feel like going anywhere this morning.

But so what? She knew she had to go out there. She took a stack of flyers, jumped in the car, and headed back to the Haverford Reserve Dog Park. It had been lucky for us before. Maybe it would be again today.

My first stop was the bank. My guys don't appreciate rubber checks. As I was driving away after transferring some funds, my cell phone rang. Normally, I'd just let it ring. I have seen too much bone-headed driving due to phone use to want to add to it. But if the call was about ZeeZee, I couldn't afford to ignore it. Time is of the essence in responding to a sighting.

I picked up the phone.

"Hello, hello; is this Katie?" a man's loud voice asked.

"No, this is Michael. Who are you?"

"We've got your dog cornered! Your dog is ZeeZee, right?"

"YES! *YES!* You've got ZeeZee? *Cornered?* Oh my GOD!" A surge of one hundred-proof adrenalin escaped from wherever it is normally stored to flood my synapses and blast my brain. I sat bolt upright in my seat and swerved to the curb. Now was no time to be doing two things at once.

"Yeah, yeah, we got her! She's boxed in. We can't get too near her; she might bite us, she's pretty worked up. You gotta come over here as soon as you can and get her."

"Where are you?" I was practically twitching with excitement.

"You know where the Quadrangle is?"

"Yes, I do!"

"Well, we're by the cottages at the Quadrangle. Hurry up!"

"I'm on my way!" I needed to be told to hurry like a starving man needs to be told to eat. I seared some rubber onto the asphalt as I peeled away from where I was parked. With one hand on the wheel, I called Katie. Five rings later, I got her voicemail. Unbelievable. Twenty times out of twenty, whenever I called Katie, she would answer. She never lets the machine take the message. And now, *now*, when reaching her was of utmost importance, she didn't answer. I couldn't imagine why. Maybe it was some kind of technical glitch. I hung up, waited a minute, and tried again. Same result. This time, I left a message.

"Katie! Where are you? They found ZeeZee! We've got to get her! I'm my way. Call me!"

It was a fifteen minute drive from where I was to where ZeeZee was cornered. The Quadrangle was a retirement village situated on seventy-four wooded acres that bordered one side of the Haverford Reserve. I had never set foot on its property, but had seen it from the road during my search, both while driving and walking. It had an array of stately brick buildings housing its administrative offices behind a cobble-stoned circular driveway that opened out to the street. There were some cottage-like structures way off to the left, and I immediately thought of them when the man mentioned where ZeeZee was trapped.

As I sped towards them, I indulged in the thought that in twelve short minutes, the object of our searching for twelve long days would be resting in my arms and trying to eat my nose. It hardly seemed possible. But it made sense. The Quadrangle was just a little bit outside the triangulated territory where ZeeZee had been sighted this whole time. She could easily have hunkered down there. And now, finally, it looked like she was at the end of her road. She was cornered. Checkmate.

I tried calling Katie once more. Again, got her voicemail. What a time to lose one's phone; the only acceptable excuse. I called Dann. He picked up right away. Unbeknownst to me, he had already spent close to two hours that morning staking out the territory on Ellis Road we had both canvassed the day before. He had also put up some flyers in that general area. Was there no stopping this guy? When I gave him the news, he sounded just as excited as I was.

"I'll be right there! I'm just a few minutes away."

That was terrific news. Although ZeeZee's fate seemed sealed, what with a couple of guys boxing her in, one should never be overconfident. There is safety in numbers.

As I pulled into the stone-paved driveway of the Quadrangle, my phone rang. It was Katie.

"WHERE ARE YOU? WHERE'S ZEEZEE?"

I had heard Katie on edge many times before, but never like this. This was her all or nothing, do or die, everything's on the line voice. It was equal parts panic, anguish, and get-the-hell-out-of-my-way emotional ferocity.

I told her where I was and how to get there. We found out later that she had been out of touch thanks to a strap on her overalls which had managed to switch off the ringer of her phone. Laws are made and laws are unmade, but Murphy's Law reigns supreme.

I whipped into one of the visitor's parking spaces. Just as I exited the vehicle, another car screeched into one of the other spaces and Dann leapt out of the driver's seat.

"Hey, Mike! You know where she is?"

"They said she was near the cottages. That's all I know. Let's go find her!"

And with that, I jumped into Dann's car and we started down the road that led away from the visitor's parking area and towards the assemblage of town homes and condos beyond that housed the Quad's residents. Neither of us was familiar with the development's layout, and it began to occur to me that the chances that we both could be wasting time and energy looking in the wrong area were pretty good. The place was huge. We needed some orientation. If I had been thinking clearly, I might have stopped into the administration's office to see if someone could guide me to where their employee had ZeeZee cornered. That would have been the thing to do, if cooler heads had prevailed. Unfortunately, the only heads prevailing were the feverish ones of Dann and me. And we were on a tear.

Dann slammed on the brakes as we came upon a fork in the road. To the left there were some tennis courts; to the right, more houses. I jumped out of the car.

"You go left, Dann. I'll go right. Call me if you see anything."

And with that, I took off running. And yelling my head off for Zees, of course. Old habits are hard to break. As I was dashing around, I saw a golf cart approaching me, with a uniformed woman at the wheel. She drove right up to me, and, with a worried look, asked if I was Michael.

She had news.

"I'm sorry, but your dog escaped."

Escaped. My dog. Escaped. The same failure to comprehend what was happening that I had experienced in Ocean Grove was now hitting me again. What did she mean, *escaped?* ZeeZee was boxed in! Her colleague had Zees cornered! He had called us! He was just waiting for me to show up and grab her! My heart, which had instantaneously made the journey from my chest to my throat when the call came in, now plummeted to a new location—my stomach. This couldn't be happening again. To be minutes away from a fresh sighting, only to be too late. ZeeZee was supposed to be surrounded. What did this woman mean, escaped?

She told me what she meant. Apparently, the picture my imagination came up with as a result of the phone call was way off. I had envisioned a garage of sorts, with the door retracted, and ZeeZee running back and forth against its far wall, barking furiously, as two men guarded the opening in case she made a break for it.

Boy, was I off. The woman in the cart set me straight. Someone had posted a flyer with ZeeZee's picture and information on a community bulletin board. Residents and staff were well aware of her, and keeping an eye out. This morning, Sean, a security officer making his rounds, saw a small black dog running alongside his car. He immediately recognized ZeeZee, and, when the opportunity presented itself, turned his car suddenly so that her way was blocked and she had to back up against a stockade fence. A coworker pulled up in another car and closed off the other end of the fence. ZeeZee seemed to be flummoxed, and began barking and snarling at the both of them, while holding her ground. That's when Sean called me. They didn't want to risk getting any closer, but felt confident they could keep her captive.

Which they did for a short while. Just until a UPS truck came barreling up and stopped right between the both of them. Whether due to its laboring engine or to the man in brown exiting with a mountain of boxes, ZeeZee got spooked and made a dash right through the gauntlet to vanish behind the hedges of a nearby town house. That was the last anyone had seen of her.

The cart lady started apologizing, which was silly, because it wasn't her fault. She was just the messenger. It wasn't the fault of the two employees who cornered ZeeZee; they were just trying to help. It wasn't the UPS guy's fault; he was just doing his job. And it wasn't ZeeZee's fault. She was just doing what she did every other second of her life—acting out of instinct. It was nobody's fault. Nobody, except, that is, for the pet sitter. His epic fail twelve days ago was the original sin, and the stain of it was still affecting all of us to this very moment.

I thanked the lady, turned, and found myself running like a madman through the streets, homes, and grounds of the Quadrangle; yelling out for ZeeZee the whole while. I didn't know what else to do. She had to be somewhere nearby. She had fled only minutes ago. I didn't want this to end like all of the other close calls. Time was running out… hers, and ours. There might never be another sighting, another chance.

I ran past some lawns, down a slope, and found myself on a path that circled around a small, beautiful lake, complete with a bubbling fountain. Here and there, residents—singly and in pairs—promenaded slowly around its perimeter. The idyllic setting reminded me of the quaint, perfect little village featured in the cult TV series The Prisoner, from the sixties. The golden sunlight glinted off the jewelry on the fashionably coiffed and attired ladies as they strolled about, canes in hand. The tableau was the picture of utopian bliss. Only, just as in the television show, something was not quite right. Something was amiss.

It was me. The middle-aged, maniacal trespasser, running around yelling strange words at the top of his lungs. As far as departures from the Quadrangle's normal routines went, this one had to rate right up there.

I was not unaware of this. Even as I strained to find ZeeZee, some vestigial sense of social propriety let me know that I was making a scene. Disturbing the peace. Maybe even causing a few folks to call the main office. But I didn't care. And I actually didn't think the residents really cared, either. Normal routines are overrated. The well-ordered habits of the men and women who lived in this community no doubt continued with very little disruption or change, day after day. That guaranteed regularity probably played heavily in their decision to live here. But this was exciting! A long-lost dog on the loose in their own back yard! A loud-mouthed man running around loose after it! This was something to talk about at lunch. Maybe even for a few days!

I remember the looks I used to get from the residents of the assisted-living facility where my elderly aunt lived when I came to visit. If you were under sixty, you could feel like a celebrity. Everyone was so eager to communicate, to make a connection, especially with anyone from an age bracket different from theirs. And although routine and stability may have been what had drawn them to this place, it was departure from the same that they secretly craved. Especially Life in its messier manifestations. In that respect, I did not disappoint.

I was about to approach a white-haired woman walking her Pomeranian to ask if she had seen a little black dog running about when I saw the figure of another man zigzagging across the landscape in a half-trot and heading towards me. It was Dann. He had run across Sean, the security officer, and learned of ZeeZee's escape. Dann's reaction was the same as mine. He had parked his car and sped as fast as his damaged lungs would allow through the Quadrangle grounds, ending up at the lake, as I had.

I didn't like hearing that. Dann shouldn't be running. He knew that. As desperate as I was to find ZeeZee, I didn't want it to be at the cost of another collapsed lung. That would be terrible. Dann did his best to assure me that he could take it; that he had built up his respiratory reserves enough to take on the extra activity. I had to believe him. The time to doubt him had long since passed.

As we commiserated, the golf cart lady came zooming up to us, again with some news. Apparently, Zees had been sighted fleeing from the lake area, where we were, and going towards the fence which separated the retirement village from the Haverford Reserve. It was a high, broad-paneled fence, which lay behind the backyards of the homes ringing the perimeter of the Quadrangle and stretching all the way from Darby Road to the far reaches of its border with the developed portion of the Reserve's grounds.

The stakes were now immeasurably raised. First Zees was cornered, then she escaped, now she was headed for the border with the virgin forest of the Reserve. If she found her way into the Reserve, she would be gone forever. We HAD to find her, pronto. It was now or never.

Dann said he was going to drive over and look for ZeeZee in the grouping of houses that lay beyond the lake and its manicured banks. I realized it was high time that I called Katie and broke the bad news to her. I knew she would take it hard.

Katie had just arrived at the visitor's parking lot in front of the Quadrangle's main building. She parked, got out, and, in keeping with the mindless example put forth by Dann and me, started zigzagging down the asphalt shouting ZeeZee's name, not having a clue as to where she was going.

That's when she got my call. She stopped in her tracks. For a moment, at least. A wail went up, audible to every resident of the Quad, even without their hearing aids. A keening shriek that could wrest a raven from its flight. And then, episode over, she was right back on the case. She said she'd meet me at the lake. She had no idea where that was.

Luckily, a car was approaching her. She stepped in front of it, waving her arms frantically. The elderly motorist braked in time, and she and her companion rolled down the windows to see what this crazy woman wanted. Katie—excited, frantic, and close to tears—pleaded that her dog had been lost, then found, then lost again, and that she had to get to the lake. Could these ladies possibly take her there?

You bet they could! The Golden Girls were on it! They told her to get in, did a three-point turn, and headed back in the direction from which they had come. That's when Katie realized her mistake. Apparently, these senior citizen versions of Thelma and Louise knew only one way to give chase—slooowly. They cranked their Lexus up to four miles an hour and kept it there. Katie would have left them in the dust if she had just kept running instead of climbing in. Her sense of frustration, helplessness and increasing anger grew to such a point that when they stopped in front of the lake, she shot out from the car like a bull entering the Plaza de Toros. She charged down to the water's edge, where we met.

There was no consoling her. As hard as it had been for me to learn that ZeeZee was on the loose again, I knew it was much worse for Katie. And yet, as distraught as she was, I could see she was making a huge effort to keep it together. ZeeZee had to be somewhere near us. Time was, yet again, of the essence. We had no choice but to spread out and cover as much ground as we could, in as many directions as we could, hoping that this time, despite all of our recent history, ZeeZee would respond to our call and come to us.

I have already established that Katie and I were a bit mad, performing the same actions again and again and expecting a different result each time. But never underestimate the value of a little insanity when it comes to finding or rescuing a lost pet. The animal is already half out of its mind. Maybe if we could join it by straying outside our own normal mind-set, a reunion might result. We would be the test case.

It was decided that Katie would continue on foot on the path around the lake and towards a more thickly-wooded area that neared the Reserve. Right away, she encountered two matrons who were excited to share that yes!, they had, indeed, seen a little black dog running around! They weren't sure where it was headed, but they had seen it. This report breathed new life into Katie's spirit, and she continued running up the path, announcing to ZeeZee and the world that Daddy and Turkey were here.

Actually, "Daddy" had returned to his van, and I was cruising slowly down every lane and through every huddle of houses within the Quadrangle's development. Their exteriors looked beautiful and picture-perfect on this gorgeous sunny day. The only thing that kept them from representing the apex of American domestic bliss was, perhaps, the presence of a dog. A small, black, aggressive Chihuahua dog, to be exact. Without it, the houses just looked empty.

After a while, as I was driving by one of the property's perimeter roads, I caught the sound of a man's voice over the noise of my van's engine shouting something unintelligible. I slowed down and poked my head out the window, the better to hear what was going on. It was silent for a few moments. And then I heard it again. A man's voice, yelling. This time, I could make out the words. I couldn't believe them, but I could hear them. Words I never thought I would hear, although I was straining to do so for so, so long. And if true, my life was about to change.

When Dann left me at the lake, he went back to his car and drove to the area near the fence towards which ZeeZee had been seen fleeing, according to the woman employee. He parked, got out, and started walking along the fence which ran behind the backyards of a long row of houses. He saw an opening in the fence and stepped through it. He was now basically hiking along the outer flank of the woods of the Reserve, moving more slowly due to the thick underbrush.

Dann had spent time exploring these woods ever since he was a child. Growing up in the area, he had spent countless hours, by himself and with friends, discovering its secrets. The fact that ZeeZee had gotten lost in what was basically his home turf was partly what motivated Dann to volunteer his energies so generously. Katie's story touched him when he heard it at the dog park a week ago. But the fact that our Zees could be hiding out in the remote, wild spaces he knew so well also spurred him to help. He was the perfect guide at the perfect time.

After walking slowly for a little while, Dann stopped to take stock of his surroundings. He stood there quietly, taking in the breeze, the smells, the sounds, and breathing regularly. For some reason—he didn't know why—he turned around and re-traced his steps. When he came back to the opening in the fence, he continued past it, going in the opposite direction. Several yards further down, he stopped again. This time, it wasn't due to his ears and nose. This time, it was due to his eyes.

And although their acuity had tested in the 20/20 range, he still had trouble believing them.

There, ten feet away, huddled in a small black ball with her back against the base of a cement barrier wall, lay ZeeZee. She was looking at him… not moving, and not seeming scared. Dann's first subliminal impression was that she was like a lamb. An angel lamb, even. She seemed peaceful and inquisitive, as opposed to aggressive. She also seemed tired, and must have in fact been utterly exhausted. The docile creature laying there, taking in this strange human, was not the same fierce hellion who had escaped the pet sitter and raced cars down the middle of Ellis Road twelve days ago. Dann wouldn't have been able to get anywhere near that dog. But twelve days of surviving in the wild, coping with the elements, sleeping who knows how fitfully, and expending her already meager caloric resources had taken their toll. She was beat. She didn't run away. Perhaps she couldn't. She just lay there, watching him, as if to dare: your move, Jack.

I am forever indebted to whichever of the Fates that had placed Dann if front of ZeeZee as opposed to me. That's because I would have done exactly the wrong thing. I would have yelled her name out at the top of my lungs and come crashing through the brush towards her with my arms extended. Precisely the sort of behavior that Gina, the wildlife tracker, had cautioned against several times. Didn't she warn us that our loving pet had by now probably morphed into a different creature as new instincts emerged in her struggle to survive? Wasn't that why she had never responded to our calls this entire time, even when we were close at hand? I doubt that I would have heeded any of these concerns if I had suddenly come face to snout with ZeeZee. My emotions would have gotten the best of me. Luckily, I was safely out of the picture.

Fortunately, the dog-whisperer part of Dann's brain instinctively knew what to do. Slowly, quietly, he lowered himself to the ground. Not to a crouch, not to his knees, but all the way down—belly in the dirt, eye-level with the wary bandit whose visage adorned so many wanted posters and who was now eyeing him with increasing interest. Her ears pricked up, and her neck stretched out, but she didn't stir.

Dann knew that whatever transpired in the next few moments would be critical. Everything, including ZeeZee's very life, hung in the balance. If she got spooked and took off into the woods, it would probably be all over. There would be no more sightings. We could never scope out the entire forested area; we wouldn't know where to start. And ZeeZee was getting much weaker. Staying put as Dann got close to her was proof enough. She wouldn't have remained there a week ago. But there was still a chance of a last gasp. She could still make a run for it; she was seen running just within the last hour. But for now, she had stopped, and now was the chance.

Without being conscious of it, Dann shifted from his dog-whispering mode to his reptilian core, as he basically attempted to slither towards Zees. It was no doubt

234

his first, clumsy attempt at slithering, yet somehow, he was making progress. This was met with a low growl that steadily developed into a series of snarls. ZeeZee had seen humans do many strange things in her life. Dann's approach may have been the strangest. She was used to people towering over her. What was with this dude who thought he was a snake? The nearer he got, the more nervous she became.

Dann closed in. He was five feet away. Then four feet. Three feet. ZeeZee was now extremely agitated, her snarls escalating to barks. Dann shimmied his legs over to one side to act as a sort of barrier, trapping her in. He was now almost just an arm's length from ZeeZee. Lying on his side, he slowly reached into his fanny belt and pulled out some doggie treats, which he offered to Zees. She sniffed furiously, but didn't take the bait. Dann had more ammo on him. He rummaged around and this time pulled out a granola bar and offered it to her. Again, her nose was working overtime, but her mouth stayed shut. She wasn't having anything.

Dann crawled even closer. ZeeZee started to tremble, and then to shake all over, her barking increasing in pitch and volume. She was obviously approaching some sort of instinctual moment of truth. Up until this moment, those instincts had always led her to run away. Yet now, she was either unable to heed them, or, perhaps, unwilling. Her proximity to Dann might have awakened the memory of her relationship with other humans, of me and Katie, of the love and nurturing such a bond possessed. Maybe the strange, slithering specimen in front of her could offer that as well.

Or maybe not. Maybe creatures like him were the exact reason the urge to flee existed. He could be dangerous. He could be the Ultimate Predator. Why take a chance by sticking around? Maybe Flight was Right.

It had to be one or the other. A battle was going on inside of Zees; it was obvious. Dann didn't know what the outcome would be, only that it was just seconds away. The time to act was now. In one smooth motion, he circled his arms around ZeeZee, grabbed her, and held her as firmly and yet as gently as he could against his side. And in that instant, her fate was sealed. Game over. The writhing, semi-feral runaway we had once snatched from a shelter was back again amongst the humans. And she seemed none too happy about it.

ZeeZee's reaction to Dann's courageous act was to bite him in the face, snapping at his nose and lips and immediately drawing blood. Dann's reaction to her reaction was to hold her even harder. Since she didn't seem to have succeeded in getting her message across the first time, Zees now clamped down fiercely on his thumb, giving it her all for at least a few seconds. That one hurt. A lot. But again, Dann's response was just to hug her more tightly. He wasn't going anywhere.

And suddenly, she realized, she wasn't either. It was over. The fight just left her. If he was the Ultimate Predator, well, he had won. Maybe he was going to hug her to death. Then again, maybe he was one of those nice humans, never mind the slithering. Whatever she first felt about this new situation, she now seemed to be accepting it. She had fought long enough.

Dann managed to prop himself up so that he was sitting with his back resting against the fence. In a calm, loving voice, he started talking to ZeeZee, letting her know everything was all right, mentioning her name over and over, communicating in every way he could that she was safe. It seemed to be working. The overwrought dog of a minute ago was now peacefully huddled just as she was when Dann first saw her, only this time, on his lap. The Ultimate Predator had become her Ultimate Protector

Carefully, Dann, the ever-resourceful, took a collar out from a pocket and put it on her. She didn't resist. Its presence on her neck must have activated past memories of similar harnessings, for she calmed down even further. This was familiar. She had been without one for twelve days, ever since her own had (mysteriously!) disappeared while in the custody of the pet sitter. Its return signaled a return to her old life. At last.

Once his adrenalin subsided a bit after the stress and drama of ZeeZee's capture, Dann couldn't help but notice the blood on his hand and shirt and that he could feel on his face. And the bleeding didn't seem to be finished. He started to feel a bit scared, and tried to take out his smart phone so that he could snap a picture and see how badly Zees had bitten him. He also had taken to yelling out "Michael! I got her!" every minute or so, in between consoling ZeeZee. And finally, he heard a voice in the distance, saying something in reply.

It was me. I had finally made out the words which had come garbled into my ears. They had to be from Dann. I yelled back.

"YOU GOT HER?"

"Yeah, I got her!"

Hearing that, I shut off my van's's engine, left it in the middle of the road, and started running in the direction of the shouts. I sped past a field of shrubs and towards a line of houses whose backyards were fenced off from the encroaching wilderness. Dann's yells seemed to be coming from somewhere behind them. As I ran, I felt my heart, which had already yo-yoed between joy and despair in the last hour, once again fill with an uncontainable and extreme exuberance.

ZEEZEE HAD BEEN CAUGHT!!

It was both incredible and unbelievable at the same time. Twelve long days of fruitless searching had passed. Although we didn't want to admit it, her continued absence at the end of each one of them had coalesced into an unspoken feeling between Katie and me that perhaps she would never be found. We had gotten to the point where we would have been okay with closure, never mind capture.

But now, the miracle had happened! She was found! It wasn't due to any single person or thing. It was the culmination of a myriad of efforts by a large group people, all selflessly invested in trying to get this skittish and scared Chihuahua back home. And just in the nick of time, too; for ZeeZee and for us. It wasn't something which could have gone on much longer.

I marched on until I came to a fence, and continued down the side which faced the forest. Dann's voice was very close now. A few yards and moments later, I came upon a scene which will forever be imprinted in my memory. There was Dann, squatting down with his back to the fence, holding a now squirming ZeeZee in his arms. I bent down, and he put ZeeZee in my arms. As he did so, I heard him say something about his blood, which I now noticed on his face and hand.

"Don't worry; it's my blood, not ZeeZee's" he kept saying. I couldn't believe it. Dann was taking pains to assure me that ZeeZee was all right; that it was merely him bleeding from several points, so there was no need to worry. Even as I was lifting Zees up in my arms, I was struck by Dann's consideration in assuring me that the blood was not hers, and by his disregard for his own injury. This was one extraordinary animal lover.

And then ZeeZee came at me with her tongue and her teeth, licking me in a frenzy of affection and mouthing my nose. Daddy was finally here! Where the hell had he been? Didn't matter. He was here now. She had been saved. This was not the near-feral creature about whom we had been warned. She may have been once, but that was over. Now, she was the same, adoring, Michael-obsessed Chihuahua she was on the morning we left for vacation.

Actually, not exactly the same. ZeeZee seemed smaller and was definitely much thinner. She had lost a large percentage of her body weight, and she hadn't had much to begin with. She had always been big in terms of bone structure when compared to others in her breed, but even that now seemed shrunken. Our sleek, well-muscled princess of a pooch had become small and fragile. I hadn't really given any thought to what would happen after ZeeZee was found, but I now knew we had to take her straight to a veterinary hospital. Any number of injuries or ailments, invisible to the eye, could have befallen her in her sojourns. There was no time to waste.

With ZeeZee now safe in my arms, I turned around and started running back to where I had left my van in the middle of the road. I shouted over my shoulder to Dann to please call Katie and let her know we had ZeeZee and that I was headed for the vet's.

Katie was still down by the lake. When Dann called her with the news, she reacted in the way that only she could. The shocking, unexpected reality that the search was over was enough to turn on the waterworks. Katie started running and stumbling along the path by the lake, trying to find her way back to her car through the blinding tears. A well-dressed matron with a compassionate heart stopped Katie as she drew near and asked her what in heaven's name was going on. This allowed Katie to tell her story, which both calmed her down and gained her a well-wisher. Senses restored, she continued on until she found herself back on the perimeter road, looking for me.

I had reached my van and gotten behind the wheel. ZeeZee had never been in the van before. In fact, she had never been in any vehicle without either being in a pet carrying case or being held in Katie's arms. But today was different. She had carte blanche. She jumped around from my lap, to the passenger seat, to the console in the middle. I made sure that the windows were most of the way up, in case she had any ideas about bailing, but other than that, her boarding pass was stamped "everywhere."

I started driving back towards the visitor's parking area in front of the Quad's main building. Along the way, one of the facility's security cars came towards me and flashed its lights. I slowed to a stop. The driver was a big, mustachioed man. It was Sean, who had first seen ZeeZee, tried to corner her, and who had called me earlier to report the sighting. As he looked up at my window, he saw a glowing me and a placid, greying Chihuahua on my lap giving him the once over.

"Hey, you got her!" he bellowed with a huge grin.

"Yeah, we did! And thank you so much! What you did was incredible. We can never thank you enough. We're going to take her to the hospital now." And with that, I took off. From the look on his face, I'll wager he never had a better day at work. The feeling evinced from saving a life, no matter of which species, is unique. It has to count among the most meaningful of human experiences. Can there be anything more precious or commendable?

I pulled up to the front parking area and saw Katie running towards me, waving her arms. The look on her face was a mixture of pure joy and high anxiety. Hearing Zees was caught was one thing. Seeing her propping herself up with her paws on the dashboard was quite another. Katie started to cry. This time, tears of happiness and just plain emotional release. She had looked everywhere for Zees, and to see her now was almost surreal; like witnessing something supra-natural.

"Katie, we've got to take her to a vet! She could be really ill with something; she's got to be looked at, right away!"

"I know, I know! Let's go! I'll follow you in the car."

I thought hearing that we needed to take ZeeZee to the animal hospital might have been news for Katie, but she had apparently thought about it from the get-go. We just had never talked about it.

Dann came up to my window. He had been trotting behind my van ever since I had taken off with Zees. Somewhat gingerly, I noticed. And suddenly I remembered about his affected lungs. How he had managed to do everything he had done so far, including just now capturing ZeeZee, I didn't know. But I could see it came with a cost. I hit the brakes.

"Yo, Dann! Are you okay? Please, take it easy! Don't run!"

Dann waved me off. "I'm okay; don't worry about it." This coming from a man still bleeding from the bites courtesy of my dog whose life he just saved.

I knew there was a vet hospital somewhere nearby, but wasn't exactly sure how to get there. I asked Dann if he knew where it was and he just said to follow him. He jumped into his car, which was parked in the visitor's area, and we formed a caravan: him in the lead, me and Zees behind, and Katie, who had jumped into our car, bringing up the rear. Dann said it was about ten minutes away.

I had a hard time keeping my eyes on the road. I just couldn't stop looking at ZeeZee, who was alternately sitting between my legs and bouncing off and onto the passenger seat. The trauma and fear which had always accompanied her inside any moving vehicle seemed to be entirely absent now. Perhaps its terrors paled compared to what she had just been through. She was obviously happy and excited. As was I. Beyond happy. Filled with an indescribable joy, more like it. The impact of what had just happened, now that the initial shock had passed, hit me in the gut and then started in on my tear ducts. Here she was! Our little weenie dog! ZeeZee! Back! Like she had never been missing; like the past twelve days had been a bad dream. The gaping hole in my heart, through which so much of my peace of mind had recently drained, was instantly healed. Just looking at her and knowing that she had been saved, that she would no longer have to suffer the hardships of surviving on her own, that she would again be showered with love and care, made my world right again.

Maybe that showed how far I am from the Buddhistic ideal of Detachment. If I had just witnessed and accepted whatever happened every day of her disappearance without judgement, then perhaps I would have taken her recovery in stride as well. Go with the Flow. Who knows? The way I saw it, though, I *was* taking her rescue in stride; only my stride was a wild-eyed, flat-out sprint towards utter joyfulness. I'll take bliss wherever I can get it.

I followed Dann as he made a right into the parking lot of the animal hospital. I scooped ZeeZee up in my arms and held her tightly before I exited my van. There was no way in heaven or hell that our little escapee could do it again, if some perverse impulse so moved her. I had her, but good. I got out and headed straight for the door, Katie and Dann following behind. Once I entered the lobby, though, Katie took over. My tendency would have been to politely wait until the staff stopped joking with one another or waiting on other customers before explaining our situation.

The heck with that! Katie made a beeline for the woman in charge and announced in no uncertain terms that they now had a full-blown emergency on their hands. Code Blue everyone! This new patient had just been rescued after twelve days alone in the wild and she had to be looked at RIGHT AWAY! In terms of triage, ZeeZee was Patient 1, 2, *and* 3! Move over, puppies and kittens! Animal ER was about to swing into high gear.

To their credit, the staff responded immediately. They took me and ZeeZee into a room and summoned the on-duty veterinarian, who came right away. Katie stayed in the lobby because local members of team ZeeZee had started to arrive. As soon as she had gotten in her car at the Quadrangle to follow me, Katie had made a group call to all the volunteers to let them know that we had found Zees and were taking her to the Keystone hospital. In no time at all, Sharon, Randy, and

Ginger had joined Dann in the lobby. It was while Katie was telling them the story of how we found Zees that it happened.

In the examining room, through a pair of closed doors, I heard it. A loud, penetrating cry issuing from some deep pit of the soul and reverberating out into the material world in waves of gasps and wails. The dam had finally burst. The battered, psychic facade that Katie had erected to allow her to function as the general who every day marshaled the forces, human and technological, to continue to look for and bring home our lost loved one, finally collapsed. There had been fissures before, but now the entire edifice crumbled. She had no more need of it. And she started crying like a baby. All of the pain and suffering, fear and frustration that she had been holding in was released. One does not experience or witness soul tears like that very often. They can cleanse to the core.

They were also, apparently, contagious. Ginger came in the examining room, weeping openly. She had never seen ZeeZee before, but looked upon her now with the love and tenderness of a member of the pack welcoming back a long-lost sister. She was also crying for Katie; touched by the relief, joy, and gratefulness for the miraculous rescue that was expressed in her cries. I think even some of the bewildered staff were starting to sniffle.

Randy also came in to check out the little banshee he had been driving around looking for the past several days. As a passionate and devoted lover of dogs, he had been involved with many other search efforts for lost pets in the past, but I'm not sure how many had been as protracted or as ultimately rewarding as this team effort to find ZeeZee. If it takes a village to raise a child, it takes a clan to find a pet. A special clan. One whose members share an almost genetic predisposition to regard any lost, suffering, hurt, or abused animal as reason to exercise and give of their own humanity. Doesn't matter who "owns" the animal. In the end, none of us do. We are but stewards, and for this special clan, stewardship extends not just to creatures they them-selves nurture, but to any that need it.

Dann came in to see ZeeZee one more time before he had to leave. He was going to go straight-away to another hospital; this time, one that treated humans. His wounds needed tending to. We would later get a call from the hospital asking for proof from our vet as to whether Zees was current with her rabies shots or not. Luckily, she was. If not, poor Dann would have had insult added to his injury. But he would have been okay with that. It was all worth it, to get ZeeZee back. Any of the volunteers would have done the same thing, but it was Dann who saved her life and salved our souls. I'm sure it was a moment which will live as long in his memory as it will in ours.

Meanwhile, the veterinarian was checking out ZeeZee. The scale revealed that Zees had lost about three pounds, which was more than a quarter of her original weight. She did look shrunken. But she still squirmed and kicked about; sniffing and scouting out the room when set down upon the floor. And despite the slings and arrows that outrageous fortune had inflicted upon her, she seemed in remarkably good shape. At least, at the moment. Time might tell a different story. But for now, we were given some medications to administer to Zees for the indefinite future as well as some special-diet dog food. And with that, we were cleared to go.

ZeeZee's new comfort with motorized transport continued on the ride home in the van. She was so happy to be in my company, I don't think she even really noticed she was a passenger. Her obsession with me seemed to have returned full force, maybe even stronger. That was okay. My own feelings towards her had grown much deeper during her absence. If you don't know what you have till it's gone, then you really know what you have when it returns.

From now on, things would be different. No more feeling cross when ZeeZee insists on interrupting my viewing of a movie right at the climax because she wants to go outside. No more impatience at her indiscriminate barking when I know she's just trying to protect me. No more annoyance when she prods me to the edge of the mattress with her paw nails so that she can stretch out on the bed to sleep. (Well, maybe still some annoyance). No more exasperation at the vet bills. (This would be very quickly put to the test.). No more surliness when I have to take her out for a walk when I'm not really feeling it.

What I'm really saying is that, in general, life with ZeeZee would continue with a heightened awareness of the preciousness and fragility of the special bond that exists between man and dog. I had never known it growing up. And was slow to embrace it as a adult. But I am so aware of it now. And if ZeeZee can find it in her heart to love me unconditionally, then the least I can do is to start losing the conditions that block my own love. It's a challenge. I'm only a human.

I parked in front of our house. Katie, who had been following in the car, did the same. For the first time in twelve days, the three of us entered the front door together. And at once, home felt like home again, and not like an empty half-way house. Katie finally got her chance to smother her little girl with hugs and kisses and not a few tears. And ZeeZee seemed as completely at home as she always had. I don't know if it was the familiar smells of the house or of us, but she was right back to being the Queen of the roost. In no time, she was back to deepening her favorite sag on top of the leather couch. And then she was out like a light.

They say animals live in the present moment; something with which we humans have a lot of trouble. I hope that it's true. I wouldn't want the twitches and whimpers ZeeZee occasionally made in her sleep to be caused by bad memories of what she had just gone through. Katie and I will never forget what happened, but ZeeZee needn't remember. Her normal psychological state was disturbed enough without adding the canine version of PTSD to it. We would do everything we could to get Zees and her life back to normal. And then maybe try to do the same thing for ourselves.

ZeeZee's behavior the rest of the day was not what we would have expected. We thought she would be ravenous. She wasn't. If anything, she was picky. Maybe her ordeal had shrunk her stomach so much that it took very little to fill it. Or perhaps she had become accustomed to subsisting on the bare minimum of food. Worst theory was that she was missing her now normal diet of voles and salamanders. But we didn't sweat it. She could eat or not eat as she saw fit. Likewise her bowels situation. She could go or not; up to her. She didn't. So be it.

It seemed she was just more than content to simply hang with us. The feeling was mutual. Katie had a lot of phone calls, tweets and text messages to make, delivering the good news and thanking all of the wonderful folks who had played some part in this miraculous turn of events. Literally hundreds of people who had been following the details of the search daily on ZeeZee's Facebook page and via tweets wrote to express their joy and congratulations on her rescue. Her story touched the hearts of people whom we had never met nor would ever meet.

I set about doing the usual household chores— straightening up, helping Katie make dinner, washing dishes. All under the watchful eye of my Shadow. You would think it would be us keeping extra watch over Zees, paranoid that she might take off again while in the backyard, or darting through the door when I opened it to take out the trash. It's like we discovered we had a winning lottery ticket in our hands. Our success in handling a million other pieces of paper was no guarantee we couldn't lose this one. ZeeZee had become so much more precious in our hearts. But in reality, it was she who was doting on us. She had won the lottery for the second time. The first was when we rescued her from the shelter before her Deadline. And the second when we did the same, only from the wilderness. There would be no third time, God willing.

When it was time for bed, Zees was up and under the covers before we got there. Highly unusual. I wondered where she had bedded the last eleven nights. Maybe nowhere. Maybe she had become nocturnal… staying awake to keep on guard from the creatures of the night and catching dog naps during the day when she could. We didn't know. And would never know all that had befallen her. We only knew what was happening Here and Now. ZeeZee's turf…the Present. The only place Life goes on.

At Present, our much-loved, long-lost, and loudly-snoring Chihuahua was cradled between my legs under the blanket. Normally I would have ingloriously shunted her off to the side, the better to sleep myself. But now? Well, I'd have to get used to it. I'll make the best of it, as she had, for so long. In the meanwhile, instead of counting sheep, I started counting my blessings. Finding ZeeZee took over the number one spot. Somewhere between my gratitude for appreciating classical music and still having most of my hair, things got hazy and

I fell asleep. Whether I snored or not, like ZeeZee, I'll never know. The important thing was, she was there the next morning.

CHAPTER FOURTEEN

We awoke at the usual time the next morning and returned to our usual routines, almost as if the ordeal of the previous twelve days had never happened. Life can be like that, can't it? Soaring one day, sinking the next. The human condition in a nutshell. Hindus call it Lila; the ever-changing play that is part and parcel of life on earth. We can be its victim, or its observer. During our search for ZeeZee, I had been both. But, to be honest, mostly the victim. I've still got a long way to go.

There were, of course, extra snuggles, kisses, and caresses sent ZeeZee's way. It was only natural. She had been taken away from us for twelve days, and almost for forever. Finding her gently snoring between us was both old and new at the same time. She was spoiled before, but that promised to be nothing compared to what lay in store for her now. Our Prodigal Chihuahua was now our Pampered Princess.

But the usual routines didn't remain usual for long. My feeling that time would tell whether or not Zees was in good condition proved prophetic, although not in the way we would have wished. On her first walk on the leash, ZeeZee vomited an extraordinary amount of runny, yellowish liquid. A trip to her regular veterinarian, as opposed to yesterday's emergency examination at the nearby animal hospital, was immediately made. Additional medications were prescribed and administered. We crossed our fingers and hoped for the best.

But problems persisted. The next day, we were alarmed to see ZeeZee deposit a red, stringy cord whose semi-technical name, we later learned at the hospital, was "raspberry jam." It looked like it sounded. It happened during a walk, and as soon as Katie saw it, she swept ZeeZee up in her arms and ran home. The bloody stool stained her shirt, and there is no color under the sun more prone to shaking her sensibilities than the dried scarlet of errant blood.

We sped over to one of the area's premier animal hospitals, fifty minutes away. ZeeZee cried all the way; her fear of motorized transport had returned with a vengeance. The visit was the first of a half dozen over the next few months, along with more visits to her regular vet. ZeeZee now had her own gastrointestinal specialist. Katie and I became experts at delivering the contents of numerous syringes twice daily to a rebellious patient. Underlying health issues had been brought to the fore because of all Zees had been through.

ZeeZee was eventually diagnosed with irritable bowel syndrome and severe food allergies. She has to remain on a strict diet for the rest of her life. No more turkey teriyaki treats. No more morsels of hot dog surreptitiously slipped to her by yours truly. No more bits of egg, chicken, steak or cheese. Yikes! Could any dog endure such deprivation? Was it possible that ZeeZee's infatuation with me had nothing to do with my intoxicating pheromones and sterling character, but everything to do with the steady trickle of taboo treats I slipped her under the table? It was a depressing thought. Now the trickle was taboo. Zees would just have to make do with bland but beneficial hypo-allergenic offerings. So long, junk food.

Katie predicted that it would take a long time for ZeeZee to get healthy again. Once again, she was right. After several months, Zees returned to a sleek but solid eleven pounds. She still needs three medications administered daily, and if a dose is missed, there could be severe consequences. But we're on it. Believe that. For a while, some of her medicines made her more thirsty than normal, with the result that she drank a lot more water, requiring midnight trips outside so she could relieve herself. The observation that dogs are like little kids who never grow up never seemed more true. Eventually, her system became more regular, as did our sleep.

Recently, we had a big scare. I was in the office, Katie in the bedroom, ZeeZee, we assumed, somewhere in-between. Suddenly, we heard the sickening sounds of ZeeZee falling head over paws from the top step of our staircase all the way down to the bottom, landing with a frightening thud and then silence. Thankfully, she was none the worse for wear. That was the last time she climbed the stairs. Ever since, either Katie or I will carry her up and down in our arms. We are determined never to hear that sickening sound again.

Zees has gotten harder of hearing, dimmer of sight, and whiter of fur. Not that different from me. She suffers from a collapsed trachea, causing her to heave and breathe in a way that resembles honking. Between the honking, the snoring, and the wheezing common to short-muzzled mutts, she sounds a bit like my work van. But she still moves around like a young dog. Barks and sasses like one, too. We were at the vets a week ago, and the doc was impressed at how well ZeeZee was doing, all things considered.

We did have a small scare with her though, also last week. Katie was walking ZeeZee in hopes she would cooperate and do Number 2, as we needed a sample to bring with us to the vet's office. Breaking from tradition, ZeeZee complied, and in trying to bag her semi-solid offering, the leash slipped out of Katie's hand without her being aware of it. The next moment, she turned around and discovered, to her horror, that she had no leash and no ZeeZee.

She looked up and saw that ZeeZee had crossed the nearby street and was racing down the sidewalk like one of those greyhounds streaking after the fake rabbit at the track. Katie screamed after her and started running, but Zees didn't let up. Luckily, she suddenly came upon a man exiting his car. She stopped and started barking at him. He sussed out the situation right away, and was somehow able to plant his foot on the loose leash and keep Zees there until Katie was able to relieve him.

The urge for going apparently still lives within ZeeZee's heart. The human end of the leash from then on has been affixed to our wrists in what only can be described as a Gordian knot.

Right now, she's on my lap, forcing me to type with one hand because she's sleeping on the other. Katie and I have yet to go away together for more than a day or two at a time since Zees was lost more than four years ago. We just haven't found anyone consistently available with whom we feel confident leaving her.

ZeeZee is even more enamored of me today than she was in the past, if that's possible. Her eyes follow me everywhere in the house. If I have to do some work in the basement, where she is not allowed, she will keep a lookout from the landing, just in case zombies show up. Whenever I come in the door, she gives me a hero's welcome. On our bed, she has generously allowed me to retreat from the precipice and sleep more in the center. But only with her curled up beside me.

And I am definitely more enamored of Zees. When I think back on what happened, and how it all might have ended up differently, I marvel at the miracle her presence in our lives represents. We were so very lucky. Just how lucky I am is something I have the rest of my life to try and realize, independent, even, of ZeeZee being found. Existence is short, fragile, terrifying at times, and beautiful. I want to be as aware of its preciousness as I can.

We had a party at a restaurant for all of the volunteers who had pitched in and been so incredibly helpful. People came from three counties and two states. Most were already engaged in new searches for other lost pets. The more I got to know these people, the more I realized that for them, this was a calling, almost a vocation. Perhaps they had a choice in it, but I doubted it. Their deep feeling for the wonderful creatures who bring us such unconditional joy direct them to do whatever they can to help. To our great good fortune.

It was good to see the team. Tammy made the drive up from Delaware. As per usual, her household was filled with her own menagerie, plus new fosters and rescues. The organization she founded—Peace, Love, and Doggie Paws—continually expands the animal rescue and adoption efforts so close to her heart. Her work has comforted the hearts of those on two and four legs equally. One on three legs as well. Tammy is a force to be reckoned with, and she will always be the Patron Saint of Lost Pets in our spiritual calendar.

Sharon insisted on funding the party, and declared that shedding her marital status had the welcome boon of freeing her up to be of even more service to needy creatures everywhere. No volunteer put more miles by foot in searching for ZeeZee than Sharon. Rain or shine, she was fully committed. If only every person had a tenth of the caring Sharon has for suffering animals, we might no longer need the SPCA. Her heart is huge.

Michele and Kevin managed to pull themselves away from their current household of seven Chihuahuas to make an appearance. They depart from them frequently, in fact, whenever the call for volunteers to look for lost pets goes out. Both of them repeatedly gave of their time and energy to search for Zees, and we are deeply thankful to them.

Randy, the mostly invisible but incessantly scanning road warrior, came with some sad news. His beloved Jigs, a German Shepard rescue, had not survived her recent ailments, despite a go-fund-me campaign he had organized on her behalf. In her memory, a new rescue dog is now by his side; as is befitting for a now full-time employee of the county's SPCA. Go, Randy!

Dann left Franklin home and instead came with the new love in his life, Becca. The two make a great couple. What is it about heroes that women find so attractive? Katie's a Dann fan. Much more than that, actually. She's feels like she could never repay him for his extraordinary efforts looking for and finding ZeeZee. Especially after he belatedly informed us of his physical condition. That sealed the deal. If Dann should ever need a kidney, Katie will be more than happy to proffer one, even if she has to dig it out of me herself. He will forever be the Mann in our lives. And ZeeZee's.

Bleb's Disease continues to be a major limiting factor in Dann's life. He recently quantified its effect on his waking life and figured he spent as much as twenty five hours a week dealing with its effects on him. He has cut down the number of students he tutors and has long ago learned to live with the chronic pain and fatigue the disease inflicts. He is a man of many dreams, talents, and ambitions, yet has recognized that he may not be able to fulfill all of them due to his illness.

That is perhaps the most amazing thing about Dann; he has the wisdom to know how to be happy. He appreciates all the gifts in his life—his relationship, his house, his job, the dogs, his friends. He values and is grateful for these blessings, even if the list doesn't include great health. Such acceptance is a special and rare virtue. Dann has it in spades. I finally have another answer to the question "Who is a hero?" Simple. Dann Furia.

Officer McClure is still providing the good citizens of his township with conscientious attention to all creatures great and small. Mostly small. But still great!

Katie's aunt has had a welcome reversal of circumstances, resulting in improved living conditions and the assistance of another big-hearted neighbor.

And Katie? Well, in a word, she's great. Doting on our doggie daughter more than ever, despite ZeeZee's continued mere toleration of her. Katie has resigned herself to the fact that ZeeZee is my dog, as I have. It was never really up to us. That's what makes Katie's continued love and devotion to Zees all the more special; it's given selflessly and without expectation of reward or any gratitude. Katie may just have cracked the age-old conundrum of how to commit a selfless act! Apparently, the presence of a Chihuahua is required.

Katie is also doting on her inner self, as well. She has always been in tune with what's going on beneath the surface of events in her life, and is even more so today. The word she has used lately to describe her state of being is "molting." Shedding the old and embracing the new. De-cluttering is the order of the day, be it objects, concepts, or habits. She used to find pleasure in acquiring objects. Now she finds pleasure in disbursing them. Katie is determined to pursue only that which truly calls to her. Currently, that involves exercises utilizing different brain-wave patterns and working with crystals and their properties. I have no doubt their secrets will soon be hers to ponder and utilize.

It was while at the party that Randy shed a little light on something that Katie and I had been thinking about. Once we got ZeeZee back, and had had a little time to process all that had happened, our thoughts turned back to Mitch, the world's worst pet-sitter. How he had lost custody of Whitey, the poodle, while we were dropping ZeeZee off. How he had lost ZeeZee a few hours later, and had taken off her tags. How he had lost Macho, the other Chihuahua, just a short while later, again, after removing her tags.

This was not a good track record. It was abysmal, in fact. And when what was being lost wasn't a material object which could be replaced but a unique being who meant the world to someone, then maybe it was a business he should not be in. If there was some action we could take that might spare a dog owner in the future from going through what we went through, then we were open to it.

We looked into litigation. And discovered something disturbing. It seems that dogs, at least according to the laws in our state, are considered "chattel." Basically, objects that are considered personal property. A more enlightened legal view can be found in many other states. But a consequence of this designation meant that there would be no grounds for a financial settlement due to Mitch's incompetence. Our hands were tied.

Katie and I actually conducted another stakeout. This time, Mitch was the object of our surveillance. We hung out in our parked car a block from his house, looking for signs he was still in the dog-sitting business. We knew that his phone number had been disconnected. The Internet posting that advertised his services had been shut down. And there were several reports of lost dogs in that area in the months after we had found ZeeZee. Surely a tell-tale sign!

We did see him walking a dog on a leash one time. It wasn't a Chihuahua. We could only hope that was because no other Chihuahua had been left in his care. He seemed to have it in for them.

Randy, following his own instincts, conducted a background check on Mitch, digging up information that was already a matter of public record. The result? Our erstwhile dog-sitter had been convicted in the past of breaking and entering, receiving stolen property, stalking and harassment, and making terroristic threats, among other infractions, in a few different counties. Not the most comforting of rap sheets. Further investigation revealed that he and Sonja were two peas in a pod...she had a rap sheet, too!

Well, hey, they paid their debt to society! Everyone deserves a second chance. Some deserve a third. Maybe some even deserve a fourth, as Mitch seems to have had. But the quantity and kind of offenses attributed to him were enough to drive any thought of retribution out of our minds. He knew where we lived. We would have to be content with working through some back channels. We eventually contacted Officer McClure, the animal control officer. He told us that if a person boarded animals in that township, he or she had to have a kennel license. Something told him that Mitch didn't. But he would find out for sure. The investigation was under-way.

But to be honest, there is something more here to be said about Mitch and his wife. Their incompetence was egregious and chronic. Their efforts towards looking for ZeeZee were minimal and short-lived. And they never made any effort to contact us after the very first couple of days. And yet...and yet...it turned out that it was Sonja, Mitch's wife, who had posted flyers on the bulletin board at the Quadrangle the day after ZeeZee went missing. Not me, not Katie, not any one of the many volunteers with whom we had worked. Sonja's flyers alerted the staff to ZeeZee's plight, and ultimately provided Sean with our phone number on that Friday morning when he had Zees temporarily surrounded.

You never know. You just never know who or what effort will be the one that brings your lost loved one back to you. You can't discount anyone, or anything. You just have to try, and keep on trying, until your dog is found or your will is lost. Blame for losing ZeeZee rests on Mitch. Credit for finding Zees rests, to a degree, on his wife. Despite all that we suffered, we are grateful for what she did. It was one piece, an important piece, of a mosaic of contributions that led to a successful rescue.

Something else was successfully rescued as well. Katie's and my relationship. Like a blade forged from a thousand blows, this intense, all-consuming effort to find our beloved ZeeZee had tempered and strengthened us. Things had been off course for such a long time. Our tiny row home had managed to house vast distances, the chasm formed by our mutual emotional negligence. The attraction we felt as opposites had slowly mutated into alienation, with the result that we found ourselves locked in a stall. Over time, it became a stall which prohibited ascent, while somehow avoiding a crash. A holding pattern which never really got us anywhere we really wanted to go. We had been really stuck.

Looking for ZeeZee got us unstuck. There just wasn't any time for "us," our bickering, our slights. In our mutual love and searching for ZeeZee, the love we had for each other was laid bare. All that was dross and difficult melted away as we focussed on the job at hand. We had worked well together. We were a team.

And now, with ZeeZee back, we're still a team. One with issues, to be sure, but one united at its core. It's not like we don't have fights anymore; let's be realistic. Katie is as passionate and emotional as she has ever been and will always be. I'm still the stuck-in-the-mud lover of Logic and champion romantic knuckle-dragger. We're just as different as we've ever been. Co-dependency still clutters up our relationship. We still get on each other's nerves. But something changed between us during those twelve surreal, scorching and stressful days spent looking for Zees. What we discovered—or, more accurately, rediscovered—could be summed up in one word.

Respect.

Somehow, over time, we had lost it for one another. After our ordeal, it was back. A bedrock, elemental understanding and appreciation for each other's uniqueness and worth. It's the basic foundation upon which love can grow, no matter what form that love might take.

It was with new eyes that I could see Katie again as she really is. Where others might see an odd woman with an ungainly gait, I see a brave woman with a swagger. Where others see a socially awkward person, I see someone uninterested in trading banalities and unafraid to call things as she sees them. Where others see a weirdo in questionable clothing, I see an original personality dressing to please herself and not caring what others think. Katie has taken to heart Oscar Wilde's admonition to be herself, as everyone else is taken. Is that not something to which we should all aspire?

It's safe to say love has manifested in several different ways in the course of Katie's and my relationship. And who knows what shape it may take down the line? Not us. But we know that our mutual respect will be there, no matter what the circumstances. The future for all of us is unknown. But the Present, for Katie and me, is more than fine.

That's where ZeeZee lives. In the Present. I wonder sometimes if she has any memory of her time in the woods. If she does, she doesn't let on. She's right back to being my Shadow, barking at dogs twice her size, snarling at little old ladies, begging for scraps (which she is sadly not permitted to have), cleansing my nostrils (don't ask), and generally being the same irascible, aggressive, cheeky Chihuahua she has always been. We are really so blessed, so lucky to have found her.

It has been argued that the dynamic between a Spiritual Master and a devotee is the ultimate human relationship. It is certainly unique; it won't be your buddy, coach, colleague, therapist or spouse who can take you from Darkness to Light, Ignorance to Realization. It takes an Enlightened Soul. And a humble student.

For ZeeZee, I am that Soul! I am that Master! Me, the most average of men. A person no one in their right mind would ever consider worthy of devotion. But ZeeZee does! It's not an exaggeration to say she worships me. I am her reason for living. She defends me every day, no matter how empty the threats. The only thing I can do when faced with such total devotion is to be totally devoted right back at her. We have taken her in, and it is our welcome duty to take care of her, to love her, and to give her the best life possible.

I have realized that pets are portals. It may not be the first thing that comes to mind while scooping out the kitty litter or on backyard poop patrol. But it's true. They connect us to our "creature" selves. It happens when we nuzzle their muzzles, when their flanks and ours are joined at rest, when we witness their instinctual love and loyalty. We long for the purity we see in them because that same purity exists within us. It's hidden, deep within, but it's there. And we get to sense it, even if just a little, in the company of wonderful creatures who have no ego, no judgement, and no duplicity.

One more thing. Unbeknownst to me, Dann captured the reunion of ZeeZee and me on his smartphone, which he had already taken out to check on his own injuries. He posted the video on YouTube. As of this writing, it can still be viewed by inputting the search words ZeeZee Chihuahua Reunion. One can see me, in my painters duds, Dann, with his bleeding nose, and ZeeZee, with her ecstatic joy and uncontrollable licking of my face. The clip was later picked up and broadcast by a cable television channel specializing in interesting Internet videos. Two of the panelists on the show asked "when's the book coming out?" Their wait is over.

Is a dog a man's best friend? I don't know. Depends on the dog and the man or woman. Does ZeeZee's love for me trump Katie's? I don't think the word love represents quite the same emotion in both of them, so the point is moot. Katie loves me in spite of my shortcomings; ZeeZee doesn't think I have any. Have to give Katie the edge there. That's major. But Zees doesn't judge me. Hmm…maybe I have to think some more about this.

Psychologists and therapists say that we need to be our own best friend. Sounds right. But it can be hard to do; we know how flawed we are, after all. Sometimes it's all we can do to just put up with ourselves. Sometimes it's all we can do to just put up with everybody else.

I think the problem is there's more to us than we usually realize. A lot more. Looking for that missing part drives much of our search for meaning. I feel grateful to have discovered that there really is something inside of us, an ocean of Peace patiently waiting beneath the waves of emotion, drama, and angst thrashing on the surface. Some of the waves we surf, some toss us about, and some sweep us away. Sometimes we float, sometimes we wipe out. But beneath them is something more—something still, powerful, and deep.

I've got a lot in common with ZeeZee. I'm lost in a wilderness, too! My peace of mind wanders in an area rife with predators pretty much on an hourly basis. It's scary out here! Always has been. I've got a well-fortified defense system to prove it. Everything could conceivably be out to get me. And by get me, I mean trick me into thinking that the waves are all that exists—there isn't anything more, nothing deeper lies beneath.

It occurs to me that, maybe, in a way, I, too, have turned feral! Maybe it's the natural consequence of having been dropped into this bewildering world of appearances from wherever "I" was previously, and taking off in a hurry in a thousand different directions, all of them offering the promise of home and none of them delivering.

And every now and then, in particularly quiet moments, I can sense something calling me. I might be afraid to face it, I might want to run, but it never stops. It's more a feeling than a voice. It can't be discerned above the voices in my head; they have to be quiet. So do my emotions. I'm free to ignore it. Or deny it. But it doesn't go away. Something is looking for me, and I am looking for something. Shall the twain ever meet?

The other scary thing about being lost in the wilderness is that the only person available to organize a search party to come and rescue me from it is me. Hardly anybody else even realizes I've gone missing! Mainly because they're lost in the woods themselves.

No, it has to be me.

Luckily, I know how to get myself home. Fortunately, it's never more than a breath away. Which is a good thing for Katie, ZeeZee, and all who know me, because I'm a better human being when I'm there. One of these days, I'm going to wise up and never leave that place. In the words of The Who, I won't be fooled again. Until then, it's Hide and Seek. Lost and Found. Living, learning, loving, and letting go. Just being a human being.

ZeeZee's home is with us. We will love and care for her for the rest of her days.

Katie's and my home is our love for each other. The dwellings come and go.

My real home is a feeling deep within. I wander from it regularly. Thankfully, it never wanders from me.

ZeeZee is still with us. And will live in our hearts forever.